By Kandace and Gregory Loewen
979-8-88759-475-0 - paperback
979-8-88759-476-7 - ebook
Glow & Gazunta Publishing

F*cking our way to Enlightenment

The true story of Maggie and Josh's
sexual and spiritual journey of discovery

Kandace and Gregory Loewen

Dedication

This book is dedicated to all seekers of love and pleasure. It is dedicated to women seeking their sexual voice. It is dedicated to singles looking to craft meaningful connections. It is dedicated to couples seeking a deeper, more passionate relationship: We encourage you to read this book together, aloud, and naked.

To our two adult sons...you may never read this book but you were the product of your parents' love and sexuality. May you derive as much pleasure from sex as we always have.

We also dedicate this to each other. This book has been a passion project that has transformed our lives. Countless hours were spent sitting on the sofa, shoulder to shoulder, talking about our stories. We didn't always agree on our recollections but we never fought once. What we became was more open and vulnerable with each other. And we discovered we both loved writing. Who knew?

Contents

Prelude

ONE • The Beginning 1

TWO • Let's Start This Party 19

THREE • Time to Play 33

FOUR • Where Do We Go From Here? 63

FIVE • From Sport Fucking to Sacred Energy Sharing 85

Photo Pages 137-141

Contents

SIX • So, Why are you Here? 143

Fifty Ways to Keep Your Lover(s) 160
aka J&M's Lifestyle Insights, Observations and Opinions

Alt Dic - an alternate dictionary 202

Sexual Preference Questionnaire 208

Resources 216

Acknowledgments...

We wish to express our gratitude to all of the players in our life story: The ones who shaped and guided us, the ones who challenged us, and the ones who made us feel safe enough to be vulnerable.

But we have the most gratitude for our editor, Fleur de Lisa Olivier. We didn't always like her suggestions, but with consideration they always made sense. Her emphatic, "But why's?" made us dig deeper into ourselves to find the answers. Her curiosity coaxed out truths that surprised us and allowed us to honor our stories. And her command of the English language erased thousands of unnecessary words. (Did we right that write? Kidding.)

From our fullest hearts, we thank our dear friend, Donna Townley, who encouraged us to be true to ourselves and share our knowledge and experience with the world. Her enthusiasm was so contagious that it turned into this book.

And thank you to our adult sons for not making our choices a thing.

Much love,
- Kandace & Gregory
(aka Maggie & Josh)

A Letter from Maggie (aka Kandace)

Maggie and Josh are our pen names throughout this book. The names were derived from a story we both read. Originally we adopted them for fun and anonymity but eventually kept them simply because we liked the look on these pages. I (Maggie) will be taking the lead to tell our story from my perspective. We have included Josh's personal thoughts on many of the events to illustrate our differing points of view.

Josh and I have enjoyed over 40 years of marriage with over 20 years in an open relationship. Our lives together have grown and expanded in the regular ways that couples do — family, home, and careers — but also through the lifestyle we have chosen.

It wasn't always easy navigating our non-monogamous relationship, but we learned the importance of respect and communication. For many people, our choices would seem risky; for us, they were exciting. Together we have created a stable and loving family life, fulfilling careers, and an ever-expanding social life. I can also say that I am married to my best friend.

I don't have a Ph.D. nor do I pretend to know more than I know. What I do have is my lived experience coupled with a desire to share my stories with others who are interested in expanding their relationships, sexuality and spirituality. I write from my heart for everyone to read and to absorb as much or as little as needed.

Writing has helped me to reflect on the paths I have chosen and to dissolve the shadows of my own personal traumas. Through reliving these moments and learning from them, this book has assisted my growth and expansion into my personal enlightenment. I have become a student and a teacher.

Although the majority of this story is written from my point of view, it is, always has been, and always will be *our* story. Josh has been by my side, every step of our life together, from the time that I was a young girl. Our life together has always been a co-creation.

My wish is that you, the reader, are blessed with self-love and compassion. May this book help you with your own self-discovery and lead you to your divine sexuality.

A Letter from Josh (aka Gregory)

When Maggie and I first began writing this memoir, it was meant to simply entertain and educate you, the reader, about the Swinger Lifestyle (aka the Lifestyle). As we recalled the many stories that filled our Swinger years, we saw our lives from a different perspective. We could see the changes and growth in our relationship and how it affected our personal development. Knowing who I had become was another step in my journey to my own personal growth.

It amazed me that after being with Maggie for over 45 years, I was still discovering new things about her. Our conversations discussing our collective memories revealed a journey that we may not have recognized if it weren't for this book. We learned a new way to communicate and truly express ourselves to each other. The process of writing as a team has brought me joy, but nothing compared to the joy of standing next to Maggie all of these years. I admire her more each day.

This story has become much deeper than our original thoughts of its direction. We discovered that lessons were concealed in many of our escapades; having the time to reflect on them has helped us to understand many of our behaviors. It took time to understand or even acknowledge "why" I made the choices that I did.

It is my desire that sharing our experiences and knowledge will help you to bring new vitality to your sexual being. I trust that you, our reader, will benefit from our stories and find your own version of enlightenment.

Introduction

The relationship that our society promotes through movies and songs is one of coupledom. Many people don't understand the Swinger Lifestyle and there is still a social stigma around open relationships. Consequently, Josh and I were encouraged by our friends to share our adventures and our insights about non-monogamy. We agreed that it was time to "come out" to allow for curiosity about other ways of connecting. Additionally, we wanted to help dispel any stereotypes about Swingers by giving examples of people joyfully engaged in non-monogamy. With the divorce stats being what they are, isn't it time we recognized that the standard relationship contract may not work for everyone?

As Josh and I were compiling our stories, we began to see a much clearer picture of our life story arc: From sport fucking to energy orgasms, our play styles have changed considerably. This book reveals how we have navigated our connection while integrating our choices into our everyday lives.

Reviewing our stories helped us to understand just how much the Lifestyle has taught us about ourselves and others. It has helped me uncover a trauma that was previously buried in my psyche. Instead of remaining a victim, that incident became a catalyst for my personal empowerment and growth. Taking control of my sexuality has strengthened my self-image and confidence in all aspects of life.

Josh and I are artists and creators who have crafted the relationship that works for us. This book will give you a very intimate look at our adventures and reveal lots of juicy insider secrets. Based on our experiences, we will offer you practices to help you navigate your own interpretation of non-monogamy. Once you have read our book, you will have the knowledge and tools to explore alternate ways to frame your own relationship.

It is a hope that our stories will give you the freedom to question where you came from, where you are, and where you want to go with the relationships that are most important to you. What are your relationship contracts based on: Tradition? Fear? Freedom? Love? This is an invitation for you to be curious and to explore these ideas in any way that may work for you. It's time to turn up the pleasure in your life.

Enlightenment:
the state of
understanding
something

The Beginning

It was a warm June morning as Josh (aka Gregory) and I (aka Kandace) stepped off the midnight train from Paris to Venice. The air was fresh but we could feel the high humidity. The water taxis waited for the tourists who were excited to get a glimpse of the most romantic place on earth. *We* were there for the sex... our first Luxury Lifestyle Vacations boat cruise, touring the Adriatic Sea with daily stops at ports in Italy and Croatia. It would be a week-long, five-star fuck fest. We would be sailing with 300 steamy, sexy couples all seeking to explore the world and our own sexualities.

The host hotel for the event was a fully restored ancient mill on the shores of picturesque Giudecca Island. We arrived and scanned the lobby for anyone that looked like they might be part of our group. Swingers were easy to recognize: attractive, flirtatious, wearing provocative attire, and having a certain presence that made people notice. As Josh and I surveyed the lobby, we played a game trying to guess which ones we would later see naked.

We had booked an executive suite and were impressed as soon as we opened the door. The room was elegantly decorated, with high ceilings and a king-size bed that was covered with a beautiful, white comforter — a little too pristine for what we had in mind.

The bellboy dropped off three large suitcases and one dedicated shoecase, which we had packed according to the nightly theme parties. With 10 years in the Swinger Lifestyle (aka the Lifestyle), we were very familiar with what we would need. I never missed a chance to dress up and show off my seductive outfits, designed specifically for each event.

A huge part of the foreplay before our Lifestyle trips would be checking the schedule for the nightly themes and planning accordingly. Josh would recline on our bed while I would assemble and model all of my skimpy costumes. Once an outfit was chosen, I would put all the items in a zip lock bag: a wig, jewelry, stockings and G-string, with a note stating which pair of stilettos/boots were required to complete the outfit. We enjoyed this little foreplay which always raised our anticipation for the trip.

The first party in Venice was the "Meet and Greet" event the organizers had arranged in one of the convention rooms. It would be our first opportunity to see who we would be traveling with, and who might be on the menu. As the time of the party approached, I slid into my white peek-a-boo minidress. The side of my dress teased, displaying my ample side boob as my ever-erect nipples strained against the fabric. I slipped into a pair of lace-trimmed stay-up stockings and donned a pair of red stiletto heels. A short, dark wig covered my long blonde hair, and I matched my makeup to complete the look. (Before you start picturing a cheap, costume wig, I'll take a moment to say that as a professional hairstylist to the stars, I designed each wig meticulously.)

Meanwhile, Josh took out the iron, pressed one of his many designer shirts, and slipped it onto his buff, 6-foot, 2-inch body. He looked like a model: tall, handsome and confident. His tight pants completed his ensemble perfectly. It was time to go meet our people!

We entered the room on time so we could maximize our opportunities for networking. We were greeted by Claudia and Pepe Aguirre, founders of Luxury Lifestyle Vacations and the organizers of the trip. We kissed each other on the lips and hugged warmly. Pepe insisted on immediately introducing us to a few new couples who hadn't been on any of the previous trips. These flirtatious introductions, typical between Swingers, were always an intersection between congeniality and desire.

I scanned the room and saw a few familiar couples including our dear friends and mentors, Nikki and Will, one of the most seasoned Lifestyle couples and experienced world travelers. I had admired Nikki ever since I met her at Hedonism in Jamaica. We greeted each other with long sensual kisses on the lips as we caressed each other's curves. Our public display of passion brought smiles to the men as they played out the thoughts of previous sexual encounters and anticipated those to come.

The room buzzed with conversation and laughter - so many couples yet oozing the sexual energy of a single's bar. The women were dressed to impress in skin-tight skirts, revealing dresses and high heels which were chosen to show off their best assets. The men were dressed in stylish attire to impress the women. Under the average marriage contract, there's the agreement to "forsake all others" and there we were, openly finding desire in the "other."

As the evening continued, Josh and I made our rounds, introducing ourselves to new couples and reconnecting with familiar ones. We had many flirtatious conversations and our few glasses of wine helped us get into the groove.

As many of the couples retreated to get a full night's sleep before the early morning boarding, we remained. We were looking to "ground and pound" as many couples as we could that coming week. It wasn't about the quality of sex, it was the quantity. We still maintained our standards but we did not need to have a personal connection; If the other two were hotties, and they thought the same way about us, it was all the connection we needed. There were more than a few occasions where at the end of a play session, we would turn to the couple and ask, "What were your names again?" A common Swingers' joke was, "You can't forget someone's name if you never knew it."

As the crowd slowly dispersed, Josh and I sharpened our fangs/eye-teeth with our fingers - our playful way of non-verbally communicating that we saw someone of interest. We honed our vision on the couple at the far end of the bar. If it sounds like we were predatory, we admittedly were, but our prey was happily consenting.

The couple of interest were stunning, with dark, toned skin, unlike our white, only slightly-tanned Canadian bodies. We approached them and introduced ourselves and as I cozied up to the wife, Natasha, we kissed almost immediately. Josh and her husband, Nigel, engaged in distracted conversation while lusting over us. It took no more than five minutes for Josh and I to invite the couple up to our suite.

We hurried back to our room to prepare it for our guests. Josh set the tone with some chill music then gathered up a few different brands of condoms and lubes. I threw a couple of red negligees over the bedside lamps to add to the ambiance. Next, we both slipped into more revealing attire.

Once the room was set up and we were dressed, it was time for the two of us to connect before our playmates arrived. (This was and is our Rule Number One: "Mates Before Dates" the Swingers' version of "Bros Before Hos.") This connection time centers us and allows us to examine how we are feeling before the others arrive. It reinforces our priorities and the paramountcy of our relationship. We knew that if at any time, one or both of us wanted to bail on a play date, an event, or even the Lifestyle, we would both be fine as our connection is the priority. That night, it was all green lights as we kissed each other with excitement.

Within moments, there was a knock at the door. I welcomed Natasha with a passionate kiss on her lips and then leaned over to Nigel and gave him the same reception. (This is our Rule Number Two: "Ladies First," that is, women make the first move. Period. This was and is a standard practice in the Lifestyle and lends itself to a more enjoyable play date.)

It seemed like the four of us were starved for each other, so it didn't take long to get into the mood. We stripped off each other's clothes as we fell easily onto the bed. I took immediate control of my scene. I reclined as I opened my legs saying to Nigel, "I'm ready for you to kiss my pussy." He smiled and stared into my eyes with lust and excitement. Meanwhile, Josh followed Natasha's toned body with his kisses, tracing her nipples with his tongue. Slowly he made his way past her navel and crested her pelvic mound.

Back on my side of the bed, the heat level was rising quickly as Nigel suggested that I roll over on all fours and let him lick my ass, a first for me. Not sure what to say, I ignored his suggestion and took the opportunity to give him a blowjob: When in doubt, a blowjob is always a good redirection. I stared deeply into Nigel's eyes as I held his cock in my mouth and began flicking his frenulum with my tongue. I sucked and stroked it but it wasn't working to get him hard. Again, Nigel said that he would love to lick my ass. I looked over at Josh for some guidance, but he couldn't see me from his position. Natasha became aware of her husband's erection status and knew what was required to get him up and performing. She moved toward me and sweetly said, "If you let him lick your ass, he will get hard for you, that's what turns him on." Once again, I looked at Josh for a sign of approval. He responded with an encouraging nod and said, "Why not?" He loved seeing me try new things and was turned on by me embracing this kink. This was one of the reasons why we enjoyed these parties and the novelty of new experiences. If I liked it, we would add it to *our* sexual repertoire.

I positioned myself on all fours, exposing myself and revealing my intimate parts without shame. Nigel firmly grasped my butt cheeks in each hand and spread me open as he pushed his tongue hard against my anus. It was such an unfamiliar sensation that I began to giggle. Feeling like I was going to pass gas (decidedly not sexy), I quickly rolled over onto my back and took Nigel's head and guided him toward my pussy. It was a fun power play between us: he wanted to lick my ass and I wanted him to lick my pussy. With his head between my pussy, it wasn't long before he asked me to roll over and let him "rim" me again. Recalling what Natasha had told me about getting him hard, I got up on all fours and once again assumed the position. Nigel put his tongue deep inside me, exploring my inner depths. The intrusion felt amazing and kinky, but the more he licked my ass, the more I felt my sphincter muscles getting dangerously loose. But it was worth it, those few licks were enough to give Nigel a solid erection. I flipped over and we were back in the game.

Meanwhile, as the sexual gymnastics were playing out on the other side of the bed, Josh was busy introducing himself to Natasha's pussy. He slowly ran his wet tongue up her legs, along the sensitive inner thighs, advancing towards the flower created by her glistening labia.

She moaned with affirmation as he softly pulled the hood back to reveal her hardening clit. Placing his lips over it, he began to gently suck it into his mouth, allowing it to just barely scrape over his teeth, sending shudders through her body. From his vantage point, her enraptured face was framed by her heaving breasts, an enticing sight.

Natasha yearned to taste what Josh brought to the party and he was happy to oblige. She repositioned herself and began her own special oral pleasure on Josh's cock. She took the whole shaft in deeply, then followed that with both of her hands firmly stroking up and down, repeating slowly. The excitement built to the point of no return and they knew it was time to grab a condom and slip it on and slip it in. Natasha reclined on her back with her knees bent up toward her chest as her hands clutched her knees. It was a great position to bang against her cervix as he watched her breasts undulating with every push.

I wanted to be closer to Josh and Natasha, so I moved Nigel to their side of the bed. I leaned over and gave Josh a passionate kiss on his lips. We frequently made contact with each other as a way of checking in. It was our reminder to ensure each other's comfort while maintaining a presence in the scene. I could feel my heart pounding and my senses felt heightened. Turning my attention back to Nigel, my mind was relentless with the desire to ride his hard cock. I gracefully straddled his lean, muscular body and slipped two fingers between my thighs and into my wet pussy. I traced his plump lips with my glistening, juicy fingers. It was my cordial invitation to fuck.

I leaned over and pressed my face into his smooth hairless chest, stopping to tease his nipples with my teeth. As my hands ran up his face, I looked deeply into his eyes. My desire flooded to the surface and I kissed him hard and fast. Nigel pulled me closer, making every inch of my skin alive with his touch. He slid his fingers inside my soft folds and felt my dripping arousal. I moaned with enjoyment as he stroked his fingers in and out, again and again until I was ready to explode.

I sat up, his hard penis protruding from beneath me. He reached for a condom and I helped him slip it onto his waiting cock. Slowly I moved my body and raised my hips to mount his raging rod. Controlling my movements, I took him deep into my wet opening, just grazing over my soft pink folds. Our eyes met again as we both smiled, satisfied that he was finally inside of me.

My hips rocked hard onto his penis. I could see that he was about to orgasm so I slowed my rhythm. I took my right hand and stuck two fingers gently into his mouth as he licked them feverishly. Withdrawing my wet fingers from his mouth, I began to rub my throbbing clit, back and forth, up and down, at just the speed and firmness that brings me closer to climax. Nigel watched with awe as I rubbed my fingers on my inner lips, taking control of my own pleasure. As I ground my hips deeply over his cock, my rocking movements were accompanied by a crescendo of moans. Faster and faster I rocked on his cock, to the sloshing of my wet pussy and the moans of my heightening pleasure.

The sounds of our imminent orgasms helped Josh and Natasha reach their own climax as they both came together in a duet of satisfied moans. I came too as I gasped, "Fuck, yes, fuck, yes!" Nigel was last to unleash his load as his eyes rolled to the back of his head. I had the sensation of flowing from one orgasm to another for what seemed like minutes. When it finally started to subside, I collapsed on the bed, cuddling into our playmates. Looking at our gorgeous new friends, Natasha with her freshly fucked hair, Nigel fully extinguished, I smiled at Josh - Venice was truly the most beautiful city on earth.

But, That's Getting a Little Ahead of the Story...

How do you become an expert in Swinging? By Malcolm Gladwell standards, it would take 10,000 hours of intense "practice" to achieve mastery. Or perhaps it's the number of partners: 200? 400? 1000? By some of these standards, Josh and I may not qualify as experts, but we do have extensive experience in the Swinger Lifestyle and have a unique perspective based on our open relationship of over 20 years.

Josh and I are a "modern" couple (code for Swingers) who are in an emotionally monogamous/sexually promiscuous relationship. Recognizing that there was something different about our relationship, we decided to share our story. Despite all of our sexual escapades (and perhaps because of them), we have created a rare and wonderful union. In the pages to come, we will take you on our journey from sport fucking to sacred sexuality, where it becomes sex for both body and mind. This was the path that we chose to take together. We made it our reality doing it the only way we knew how... our way.

Sometimes the Apple *Does* Fall Far From the Tree

Josh and I both grew up in the same small town where we were somewhat insulated from the big world. In those days, the Internet didn't exist and our worldview was very limited compared to today's bombardment of information. The idea of an open relationship or any alternative lifestyle was never discussed in our households. This kind of marriage wasn't even in the realm of possibilities.

My home was much stricter than Josh's: I wasn't allowed to wear makeup, get my ears pierced or date boys until I was 15. Through my early teens, I was involved with the church's girl's group, youth choir and Friday night youth events. Yet, I had my first cigarette at the age of 12, my first joint, beer and boyfriend at 13, and was having sex at 16.

I met Josh at church when I was 7 and he was 8. He and his family always sat two rows in front of my family. Josh was the older boy who I was intrigued and attracted to, even when I was 7. We had a connection from the beginning and five years later, we were hanging out with the Church Youth Group on Friday nights and holding hands while ice skating. I remember having dreams about marrying him, living in a beautiful house and owning a color television. At that time, that was as far as my imagination could be stretched. Shortly after that, our family decided to move to another, more extreme Pentecostal church and Josh and I lost contact with each other.

When I was a young girl, I remember my mother being subservient to my dad. She was taught by the church to love, honor and obey her husband. I grew up with two older brothers and they would boss me around constantly - even when we played together it was by their rules and their suggestions not mine. This impacted me and I somehow knew that boys and men would attempt control over me.

When I was 16 years old, I had a boss who coerced me into giving him a blowjob. I didn't realize that I had a choice to say no. So I went through my teen years and into my early 20s thinking that this was going to be a life of compromises and accepting things that happened to me as just being normal. Yet, on the other hand, I totally blocked out this sexual trauma in an effort to avoid being a victim. I never considered how this was going to impact my life as I became a woman.

When I was 17, a girlfriend invited me to Josh's surprise 18th birthday party and we had a chance to reconnect. The next day, I went over to his house for a private swim. He took me into the house, stripped off my bikini, and wanted to have sex. I told him "no" and he listened and respected me. At that point, Josh and I started dating; I felt safe, needed, accepted and cared for around him. My dad had died a year previously and, on some level, I felt that Josh would take over as my protector. Josh gave me the love and attention that my distant father never did.

Josh - I was the black sheep of my family - not because of some rebellious teen angst, but more that I didn't subscribe to Christianity as it was being taught to me. I believed in a higher power, just not the way it was described by our Sunday school teachers. There were too many holes in the bible stories for me to truly believe. I was beginning to discover my critical thinking and that "the beaten path" wasn't the one that interested me. I never agreed with the church's beliefs that sexual pleasure was equated with sin. It never made sense to me.

My parents were loving, generous people. They enjoyed a good life together and were happily married for over 60 years. Their care and respect for each other left a lasting impression on me and taught me how to treat a significant other. This I brought into my relationship with Maggie.

Otherwise, I think I was a pretty normal kid, yet Maggie reminded me that most normal kids at the time weren't having sex at 14, smoking weed and sharing it with the other kids in the Church Youth Group. So perhaps I always had the appearance of "normality" yet continued to do the things that I enjoyed behind the scenes.

A few years after we started dating, Josh and I got married. Not long after the wedding, we both realized that living in a small community was not our dream so we moved to the big city. The city we chose was bustling and had a strong art and music community. This injection into our creativity helped us to expand our own artistic expressions and broaden our worldviews.

The city exposed us to new opportunities, influences and attitudes. It was the eighties and a great time to be in our early adult years: We met people that reflected our image and it felt like we belonged; we hung out at nude beaches and gay bars; and we found careers that rewarded our expressive natures. Friends, clients, and workmates were coming out about their own sexuality and personal choices. It introduced us to a world that was new to us. The definitions of sexuality that we had been taught were beginning to erode. It was an environment of freedom to be an individual without fear of judgment. Cross-dressers and friends of all sexual descriptors became the preferred tribe. We had found our people, the ones who were open and who embraced change. We explored rave parties and anything off the beaten track that fueled our curiosity. We were learning to accept and love ourselves as well as others. That move to the city was the first big step in our evolution: We began to live life from the inside out rather than from the outside in.

When Keeping up with the Joneses is not Quite Enough

As our anniversaries ticked by, Josh and I immersed ourselves in our careers and supported each other in our chosen endeavors. It was an expansive time in our lives with the addition of kids, a great home, a dog and lots of "stuff." We carved out a place for ourselves and loved to entertain in standard monogamous ways.

As we moved into our 40's, the usual, mid-life questions lurked. Josh and I both worked in the gig economy which allowed a certain amount of freedom, both financially and socially. As artists, we felt that we had a pass to skip many social conformities. Yet despite enjoying a somewhat full life, we were getting bored and a persistent "What now?" question loomed.

That's when things changed, as they always do. It was evident in each other's body language and energy. The intimacy had declined as our energy was consumed by work and home life. When our children entered the picture, we chose to neglect some of our own desires to focus on their needs. This part of the story is not new, like most parents, we loved our kids and made sure their lives were filled with the attention, love and experiences they deserved. As priorities shifted to those small, beautiful creatures, we began to feel a strain on our intimate lives.

Twenty years of marriage provided security, love, friendship and stability, but I was looking for something more. I remember asking Josh if he would attend motivational workshops on advancing our marriage and careers, but his response was, "Why fix something that isn't broken?" I knew in my heart that nothing was broken, but I felt that something was missing.

I had already learned to navigate the male-dominated film industry before the #MeToo movement. At the time, the film industry considered "harass" to be two words, her-ass. As a female, I had to have pretty thick skin and creative ways to cope with the patriarchal atmosphere. I would listen and sometimes laugh at men's sexist jokes and would even let them touch my ass in a playful manner. Yet, unlike when I was a teenager, I didn't let them cross my boundaries. Producers knew that even the most sexist of actors could not rattle me or get me off my game. Being married also put me in the "hands off" category. Throughout my career, I would tell Josh the stories of what went on at work and he would be supportive and reassuring. He knew that I was strong enough to handle them and he never felt the need to try and save me. I didn't need saving. I had blonde hair and big tits, they'll get you almost anything.

I had an unexplainable appetite for sex and a very high libido. With my work days sometimes 14 hours long, and with so much time away from home and family, my eyes began to wander and my workmates started feeling familiar and close. I began fantasizing and the persistent flirting would make me aroused. I was curious about sexually open relationships but I had no idea how to start the conversation with Josh. I had no idea how my lust could fit into my existing marriage.

Forsake *all* Others?

I got plenty of intimacy and emotional support from Josh but I craved more sex. I loved the attention of other men - it was a real self-esteem boost, and it stroked my ego. Josh was no longer a valuable source of validation for me. He was always complimentary and supportive but I felt he was saying those things just because he loved me. I felt I needed other men to find me sexy, pretty and desirable. I needed multiple opinions. At that time, I didn't realize that I was the first and the most important opinion and Josh was the second.

Perhaps this need was linked to the relationship that I had with my father. He was a veteran of WWII, who lacked the ability to connect or show affection. He was absent in my life even before he died and didn't give me much attention, except when punishing me. Despite Josh and I creating a union of equals, I still longed for the attention of the unattainable male.

I was beginning to feel the need for more excitement and pleasure. Josh and I had a good sex life, but with both of us working full-time, we often found ourselves too tired or too busy with our children. Life was getting in the way of our libidos and sometimes we would go weeks without having sex. We would cuddle and be close, but sex fell from the list of priorities. Something had to shift and I valued my relationship with Josh too much to let that something happen behind his back.

Josh and I recognized that changes were necessary and that it was time for some self care. This wasn't about the kids, it was about us and our needs to stay mentally and physically healthy. We needed a way to make our lives more exciting and sexy. We wanted to get some of our old life back, but neither of us had a blueprint of how that would look.

Josh - Being away from your family for 60 hours a week or more can cause havoc to a relationship. And when both of you are away from each other but close to others day in and day out, they become your life. I could tell we were both becoming complacent in our relationship. My priority was to provide for the family in whichever way was required. That distracted me from Maggie and our relationship. Our conversations were about work and the times we were spending with others, not about us. I needed to get reconnected with my life partner.

The Stopgap Measure

Travel was always something Josh and I both loved. We felt that exposure to other cultures, societies and new experiences fed our love for life. A one-week "parent escape" to some place tropical, was what we needed, and we began to do it annually. It was as much a break for our kids as it was for us.

We often say that we have the "Variety" gene, otherwise known as the "Novelty Seeking" gene, that natural desire in the DNA that looks for new experiences. Some people have this variant while some people prefer the safe and familiar. As long as we had the comfort and safety of each other as our "base", we felt free to explore all the pleasurable things that the world had to offer. Those romantic adult trips allowed for some novelty and awoke the desire for more pleasure in our lives. It was that little break away from everyday life that helped us realize that we needed to look after ourselves and our needs.

It all Started in the Hot Tub

Our "first time" Swinging, began like many other stories of couples expanding their sexual relationship with others...in the hot tub. With close friends, the right music, and the right amount of tequila shots, it was an easy beginning.

April and Kirk were an attractive couple and long-time friends. They were 6 years younger than us and had a similar enthusiasm for life. The evening started as any other dinner party, but what happened afterwards opened the door for what would evolve into a new and exciting lifestyle.

As the evening progressed, Kirk sat next to me, flirting and telling me how great I looked. As I looked over at Josh, I could see that he and April were deep in conversation and the mood seemed equally flirtatious. Since Josh was happily engaged, I decided to enjoy Kirk's attention. I was used to having guys compliment my body, but it felt good that it was happening with Josh present.

I suggested that we all go and relax in the hot tub so the four of us took our clothes off and slid into the tub. This wasn't the first time we had socialized naked as we had seen them at the local clothing-optional beach. April had a beautiful, sexy body with large, natural breasts and a tiny soul patch that crowned her vulva. She had a toned, tanned body with dark shoulder-length hair that I always admired. I enjoyed witnessing a fellow goddess. I didn't feel competitive with other women and always appreciated their uniqueness, even though I had my own body issues. As for Kirk, he was fit and carried a noticeably nicely sized cock.

As we all sat in the hot tub, the conversation turned steamy. Kirk took my leg and it made me tingle as he rubbed my skin underwater. I nervously returned his touch, brushing my arm against his arm. His gaze told me that he wasn't about to move away. He was a man smitten, and I'm sure the look in my eye was equally as lustful.

Across the hot tub, I could see Josh caressing April's shoulders and playing with her long hair. He was obviously enjoying the unique direction the evening was taking. And then, they kissed, and as I watched, I became aroused as if it were happening to me.

With all the heat, April said she was getting too light-headed in the tub and needed to get out of the water. As Josh followed her out, I could see his cock was hard. They went to the couch, still visible to me and Kirk. Not one cell of my body felt that Josh was cheating on me; it was an invitation for me to do the same with Kirk.

Kirk saw this as an opportunity and moved closer beside me and then slowly slid himself under my body. My ass cheeks were now straddling his growing cock. It was an incredible compliment to feel his penis grow hard because of me. He kissed and nibbled lightly on my neck, sending tingles up my spine. I pressed back into him, grinding my cheeks into his firm cock. He cupped his hands onto my pulsing mound, sending another rush up my spine. His fingers squeezed my clit as he slowly massaged it. I moaned as he adjusted himself and slid his hard cock closer to my pussy.

My body was on fire with the attention he was giving me. I could feel his penis pressing between my lips, teasing me, taunting me. I knew I was wet and so did he; I was so ready for him. I turned to face him and eased on top of his lap, kissing his soft lips. When his tip entered me, I groaned with pleasure. When he slid into my wet pussy, we were completely present with each other. I abandoned all thoughts of what Josh was doing. At that moment I wasn't wife, mother, or daughter - I was a woman following her desire.

Our grinding and pumping created tidal waves in the hot tub and all the way up my spine. Gushes of water spilled onto the deck. I ground hard against his throbbing cock, our breath faster and deeper. When I looked into his eyes, I could tell he was getting close; I felt another wave of excitement rising through my body — we were both near the edge. As we continued our gaze, we both let out a gasp of sheer ecstasy as we climaxed together.

The afterglow was filled with silence as I slid off his lap to the seat beside Kirk. There wasn't any apparent jealousy or negativity, we were both lost in our thoughts. As the hot tub water returned to relative calm, I sensed that experience would send ripples into my marriage with Josh. The possibilities were endless and exciting.

The next time we saw April and Kirk, it was like nothing had ever happened. I wanted to hug them and tell them how much they had changed our sex life. We never played with them after that, but have remained casual friends.

When Josh and I awoke the next day, we didn't feel regret about our choice to have sex with April and Kirk. We didn't see any downside. That first time taught us a few things about ourselves and our experience: we didn't have jealous feelings, it was fun, it was exciting, it gave us a major serotonin rush, and it added to our own sex life when we recalled those steamy scenes.

Even after that first encounter, the idea of moving forward into an open relationship wasn't something that we considered. We didn't know it was an option because we lacked the model of what an open marriage might look like. Still, the thrill of an intimate encounter with other partners was very alluring.

From that first experience, we knew that extra encounters would be a bonus to our relationship, not a threat. We didn't get caught up in all the "What if's?" We knew that our relationship was solid and that there would always be a Josh and Maggie. That night set in motion the shared desire to seek out similar types of pleasure.

We are all just a bunch of
freaks
Some of us are just more
honest about it

Let's Start This Party

Sharing our bodies with others in the hot tub had an immediate effect on me. It was the first time that I could see myself finding the sexual nourishment that I craved without compromising my relationship with Josh. My imagination for what was possible was stretching: I was creating a life that was grander than a house with a color TV. Yet, I still had my doubts. The lingering question remained...was it possible to fulfill all of my desires without compromising my integrity and the respect that I had for my husband? That was the billion-dollar question.

I loved Josh being the dominant one in the bedroom. I didn't want that to change, yet my need to be dominant was escalating, and it didn't feel right to go there with him. There was an underexpressed side of myself that was the female version of the Alpha male and she was just waiting to be unleashed. She craved being the top.

Despite my hidden yearning, I still lacked the tools and the freedom to express my desires. Although I wanted to spice up my life, it would be selfish for me to have an affair. Both Josh and I enjoyed the variety and craved titillation so it made sense that all of our experiences should be shared.

Our home base was established and we both knew we were a good husband and wife team. The only thing missing was the zingy passion that comes with an extra-marital affair or a new relationship. What would a life of inter-marital affairs look like? Would we get to enjoy that "first-time" feeling over and over? Could we catch those dating butterflies in a net that we held together?

We had so many unanswered questions and although we were treading into unknown territory, we were doing it together.

Time to Dive In

Josh and I had heard about Hedonism in Jamaica, an Adult Only/ Clothing Optional Club (think R-Rated Club Med). At that time, the best way to book such a vacation was through a travel agent. When we told her about our desired destination, she raised her eyebrow. Then she checked her computer and her curiosity turned to enticement and she said, "I would love to join you." We were all titillated.

Hedonism had two resorts: Hedo II and Hedo III. Both clubs were known for their freedom of "sexpression." Hedonism II had a reputation for being a little raunchy, according to what little information we could find. Hedo III, on the other hand, was a newer club and looked a little tamer for our virgin journey. We booked a one-week adventure with warm water, nude beaches, sunny days, and loose morals. What wasn't to like?

We arrived in Jamaica at the resort around noon. We dropped our suitcases in our room, put on our beach wraps and ventured to explore the grounds. The resort was a beautiful tropical paradise, with seven pools, open entertainment areas, and white sandy beaches. The nightclub featured a clear waterslide that ran through the outer walls of the building and right over the dance floor. The resort had numerous activities with high-energy staff to entertain and lead the guests.

On the beach, we found a circus-size trapeze. We looked at each other and said, "Why not?" It was a daring mission but we were intrepid thrill seekers. Neither of us were gymnasts but there was an experienced crew to help us. The rig was a traditional circus setup with multiple towers, fly and catch bars. A large net was positioned below to catch us if we fell. After some instruction, we each took turns launching ourselves into oblivion. It was scary as hell. Even though we were both in pretty good shape, hanging from a bar, 30 feet off the ground while swinging like a pendulum uses some very different muscles. It was a metaphorical introduction to the thrills we would soon be experiencing.

One thing we both noticed while up in the air was the pounding beat of music coming from the distance. Across the resort, there was a party going on and the music was drawing us in.

We found a pool area that was nestled between four buildings. When we arrived at the party, a DJ was blasting music to energize the crowd of naked frolickers. As we approached the swim-up bar, we noticed a pair of nude women on their hands and knees on the counter. The bartenders were pouring shots down the small of their backs, through the valley of their ass and into the waiting mouths of excited recipients.

Josh and I were gobsmacked and overwhelmed by the sexual energy around us. The music was so loud and the people were so flirtatious that I couldn't collect my thoughts. Josh and I retreated to a quieter beach pool, where we could process the scene we just witnessed. We were equally aroused and trepidatious about the environment we had chosen. Serendipitously, the week we booked coincided with a Lifestyles Organization event, although at that time we had no idea what that meant.

At the smaller, quieter pool, it was easier to integrate without all the visual and audible distractions. Josh and I met a friendly couple who were tanned, very fit and nude. We were accustomed to nude beaches and had no trouble having conversations with naked strangers. We explained that we were overwhelmed with our first Lifestyle event but as Josh and I talked to them, we relaxed. Our new friends, Nikki and Will, were seasoned Lifestylers who knew many of the couples at the resort. They shared stories of their world Lifestyle travels and gave us a glimpse of what was possible.

After a few drinks, Josh had to find a bathroom. On his return trip, he stopped to get drinks for our group. As he passed by the shallow pool, two attractive women stopped him, and one of them asked, "What time is it?" After awkwardly juggling the four drinks to view his watch, the ladies decided his effort deserved a reward. I saw Josh, drinks still in hand, receiving a two-mouthed blow job from the sexy strangers. All he could do was smile and shrug at me, and try not to spill our beverages.

Later, he explained to me that the oral pleasure was his gift for giving them the time. It was over as quickly as it had begun and they giggled and continued on their way. I was taken aback by the sexual freedom the women expressed. Josh and I found it playful and fun and couldn't wait to see what else was in store for us that week.

Apparently, this kind of action wasn't rare in this environment. Nikki and Will shared a few of their crazy sexy stories that afternoon as we hung out with them. I found myself asking Nikki questions about how the Lifestyle could be integrated into our lives. They became not just our mentors, but more importantly, our good friends. We are so grateful for the knowledge and guidance that they have given us on our journey. They were the ones that invited us to our first play party...

Our (Almost) First Play Party

By 5 pm at a traditional resort, we would go back to our room for a siesta followed by dressing for dinner. At Hedo III, Happy Hour was Whoopee Hour. Nikki and Will invited us to a play party and we were equally excited and nervous about the prospect. I told Josh that I didn't know if I could handle an orgy, yet as we talked about it, we decided that YOLO (you only live once) - and as long as we were in it together, we would be okay. So, we both downed some liquid courage and decided to accept the offer.

At Hedo III, just about everyone was shaved, waxed or trimmed. Personal hygiene was equally important to us so we needed to assure that we were well-groomed. We preened a tad too long, arriving at the party 30 minutes late.

Our knock on the door was answered by Will, who was naked with a smile and a very erect penis that was pointed in my direction. As the door swung open, I saw three couples, naked in the room. They were sweaty with big smiles on their faces, as they looked over at us, "the fresh meat."

They welcomed us in. I had no idea that there would be two other couples joining us. We hadn't even met at the pool and there they were, banging each other happily. I felt like I was back on the trapeze, letting go of something mid-air while awaiting for something else that I couldn't yet see. I was deep in the discomfort of limbo. I felt awkward and politely said that we wouldn't be joining them. Josh and I turned and walked away.

Our first day had been filled with new experiences and I needed to slow things down. As we walked back to our room, I told Josh that my emotions were running high. It was all new territory and I explained that even though I was keen to start on this new part of our journey together, we needed to decide how to navigate the Lifestyle. I wanted to know more about the trapeze that I would be jumping to grab. This might take some time.

Josh - When the door to our first play party opened to reveal the naked bodies and the smell of sex, I was ready to jump in and on! To say I didn't feel disappointed when Maggie tugged me away would be a lie. Yet, I recognized Maggie's anxiety and I knew she wasn't comfortable in that space. I wasn't going to let my transitory desire get in the way of giving my wife and mother of my kids the respect and honor that she deserved. In addition, I was proud of her for not letting the lust of others persuade her into an uncomfortable situation. I kept my pouting on the inside and didn't let her see my disappointment as I knew that would be selfish of me. I also knew that more opportunities would present themselves, after all, it was only day one.

Later that evening, Josh and I met Nikki and Will for dinner. We were a bit embarrassed about our quick departure from their play party but they understood our hesitation in joining group sex for the first time. We appreciated that our new friends didn't judge us and continued to make us feel welcome. We continued our conversations openly, discussing intimate topics rarely heard amongst couples. We were becoming more comfortable.

It was the following afternoon by the pool that I spent time with

Nikki alone. She and Will had been in an open relationship for several years. Nikki was the first one to explain the "Ladies First" rule where women typically made the decisions regarding playtime. The wives would strike up conversations with potential playmates and once they were comfortable with each other, a hook-up would be arranged. At that point, there would be a trust and comfort level established for everyone involved and the men would honor their partner's choices. I liked that arrangement. It felt reassuring and comfortable because I would be in control of my body and my play partners.

My Fantasies Fulfilled

The second day around the pool with our new friend taught me the basic rule of engagement. Nikki reassured me that we were in a safe and inviting environment. The possibility of hooking up with someone new was now more exciting and both Josh and I wanted to put our new found "Swinger" knowledge into practice.

For a few years, I had a recurring dream about being with a striking, 6 foot 6 black man with large muscles and a huge cock. On our second night at Hedo III, there he was standing at the bar with a beautiful blonde beside him. He was everything I wanted and needed to fulfill my fantasy and I knew I had to express my desires to Josh. When my fantasy life intersected with reality, I had to jump on it. Literally.

I felt awkward and a bit selfish to ask, but I figured that if I just told Josh the truth about my fantasy, then we could start this open relationship on the right foot. I explained to him how I wanted to have my fantasy fulfilled and it would have to be alone with the other man. Josh said "yes" and I appreciated his openness in making my fantasy come true.

One man down, one to go. I still didn't know if that one would be willing, but we introduced ourselves to Neal and Colleen. I explained my fantasy to her and she was totally open to me borrowing her husband. It was that easy. Swingers are good sharers.

We left Colleen at the bar and the three of us walked down to the pool area. I nervously kissed Josh and left him alone on a lounge chair as I walked off with my new found playmate.

We found a dark area on the far side of the beach and I lay back on a chaise and spread my legs with anticipation. There was no small talk as Neal bent down on his knees and began kissing my pussy. As I stared up at the stars and the moonlit sky, I could feel his tongue moving up and down my clit, as he took in all my juices. I couldn't tell if it was real life or one of my erotic wet dreams.

I was so aroused and my pussy was aching for him. I played with my myself as I watched him stretch a condom over his huge cock. I had never been with someone that big before, and I wondered if he would even fit inside of me.

I continued touching myself, coaxing my dripping pussy to open to his heavily veined shaft. He entered me slowly, knowing he would need to take it gently. My body responded with shakes, and I breathed deeply, looking into his eyes.

I wanted all of him inside of me, so I rubbed my clit harder. When I relaxed and opened up, he pushed in deeper and faster. My pussy was throbbing at the sheer size of his cock. It was extreme pleasure edged with pulsing pain. My wet pussy was receiving it all.

In and out, pleasure tinged with pain. It was like Neal was helping me birth a whole new world filled with fulfilled fantasy, erotic reality, and living, breathing dreams.

Anyone could have seen us or heard us as we lay under the moonlight and this added to my excitement. Our breath united as we both exploded at the same time. There was ecstasy, bliss, and fireworks in my mind, and I arched my back as my body shuddered with energy.

Spent and exhausted, we caught our breath, reassembled ourselves and headed back to our partners. I kissed him and said goodbye and thanked him for his gift and then turned my attention back to Josh.

Josh asked me how it went, with a smile on his face. I managed to whisper, "My fantasy was fulfilled."

We continued our conversation back in our room. It was so freeing for me, knowing that Josh was excited to hear my story. I told him every detail of what happened and what I was feeling. I was able to live out a personal fantasy that didn't involve my husband but I had his blessing.

The next day, I wasn't sure how to act around Neal and Colleen. Were we supposed to hang out with them? There wasn't much to talk about. I needed to tell myself that it was only a one-night stand, just a fantasy fuck. Don't get me wrong, they were lovely people. We wanted to explore more yet felt guilty leaving them. This was something we were going to have to deal with moving forward.

After much of the day of hanging with them at the pool, I found my mentor, Nikki and asked, "What should I do?" She said, "Don't worry, he was just a fuck buddy. You can move on to another couple. No one will have hard feelings. We are all doing the same thing. We have our husbands as our soulmates/best friends and we don't need these other sexual partners for anything more than a good fuck."

Josh - Maggie sheepishly asked for my blessing. I say it that way because I feel saying "allow" in a relationship suggests ownership or some kind of authority over her. This was going to be all about her, it was her fantasy and I was curiously excited about what was to come, pun intended. The three of us left the club together and made our way down to the pool area. Maggie wanted a neutral spot and she chose a lounge chair down by the beach which offered a small bit of privacy. I remained back beside the pool as I watched them part together, disappearing into the starlit night.

It felt like forever waiting for her to return. Sitting on a lounge chair by myself, I had thoughts of self-pity but also a concern for her safety. Did I look like a loser while my wife was off fucking some guy? I had never been in that position before. What was I supposed to do? My ego was on full alert and I didn't know how to react.

Underneath all of the self-doubt, the thoughts of her being pleasured by that huge cock actually excited me. I was conflicted yet felt good that she was owning her body and sexuality. I found it interesting that I did not feel a need to "get even" by having my own separate playtime. Her enjoyment fulfilled me in ways that I was not familiar with. That was the first time I felt compersion. It took me many years before I actually discovered this feeling had a name and was a recognized psychological response.

I felt my heart swell when she came out of the darkness. It was an instant relief when she returned to me. She was safe and back in my arms.

And she looked absolutely radiant. The sexual afterglow shone from her, I could sense her pleasure and gratitude.

That first night was a good test for us and I feel we passed with flying colors. I couldn't wait to hear all about it, and she couldn't wait to tell me everything. We were hooked.

Poolside Pussy Time

I was like a kid at an amusement park. I was having so many first-time experiences at Hedo III. I wanted to try every ride! It was so freeing to watch the enjoyment and feel the high energy at the resort. I was observing all the activities happening, from body shots to women squirting, pole dancing, sex swings in rooms, couples wearing bondage outfits at breakfast, men in dresses, people having sex outdoors and group sex parties. It was a free for all, and I for one felt it very freeing.

My favorite was poolside pussy licking. It was our second day at Hedo III and I was beginning to open up and accept the Lifestyle. Everyone there was on the same page. We were all there to play and have fun. Josh and I went down to the pool that was located beside the beach. It had a swim-up bar on one side and a cave with a waterfall on the other end. It looked like a fantasy land.

As we approached the pool, I noticed half a dozen sexy, naked women, sitting on the edge, dangling their legs in the water. They were all chatting and laughing together. I love to socialize so I approached the women. What I didn't notice was that there were men in the pool with just their heads bobbing above water between the women's legs. I did notice Nikki and she invited me to sit beside her and she immediately introduced me to all the women. I felt accepted and I knew new friendships were beginning. Nikki explained that the men between their legs were all gentlemen and would always ask before approaching any lady. She introduced me to Allen, a single guy known as a Bull or a Stunt Cock. These were new terms to me. She explained that he would be invited to couples' play parties/orgies as the extra cock. Well, that sounded quite exciting to me, thinking that I may get a chance to ride that Bull. Almost immediately, Allen asked me, "Can

I kiss your pussy"? I looked over at Josh in the pool and he smiled at me with approval. I knew he was on board when he approached Nikki and asked to lick hers. It wasn't long before there would be another hot guy with his head between my thighs giving me oral pleasure. This was a surreal day for me and I was going to embrace it all. I felt I was part of a new community: Josh and I were welcomed with open hearts, minds and legs.

Don't Judge a Book...

With our newfound knowledge and confidence, Josh and I jumped into the Lifestyle and wanted more open-minded friends. There were couples of every description at the resort that week, such as same-sex couples, poly throuples, fetishists, Unicorns and Bulls. The Lifestyles Organization was one of the few organized groups back then and they catered to many different kinks and choices.

One couple caught our eye early on in the week. She was a larger lady, covered in tattoos and he had bright blue hair. They were older, maybe in their late 50's early 60's. They arrived at every breakfast buffet dressed in various bondage attire. She wore shiny latex panties and bras, he wore leather strapped harnesses, and they both wore thigh-high platform boots. Needless to say, they stood out from the rest of the crowd. Just like any other segment of society (even within the fringe groups) there is judgment about personal choices. We overheard negative comments about the couple's appearance. Because we were breaking away from cultural norms, it was necessary for us to be accepted by those within the group so sadly, those comments held us back from getting to know the other couple. I had concerns about even approaching anyone who didn't interest me sexually. We were such Newbies, that we didn't fully understand that every conversation would not lead to a hook-up. That kinky couple intrigued us, but they also frightened us a bit. We hadn't been exposed to that fetish side of society before so we didn't know what to expect if we approached them. It wasn't until the last night that we actually talked to them.

It was the end of the week and the Lifestyles Organization event was over but our reservations had us there for one more night. With most of the Lifestylers gone, the resort was filling back up. This time the group was radio show contest winners, quite a change in the guest list. The dance floor that was previously jammed with sexy, half-naked partygoers had been replaced by a room filled with wallflowers watching us getting jiggy on the dance floor.

On our way back to our room that night we came across the kinky, blue-haired couple. He was wearing a long wig, dress, heels and hosiery and was leaning against a wall like he was being arrested, legs spread and arms extended. The harsh overhead lighting gave the scene a gritty feel. His short skirt revealed his ass cheeks and his dangling manly bits between his legs. The glimmering light reflecting from his scrotum caught my attention. When we approached, his wife was positioned behind him and was attempting to take a sexy photo. We offered assistance and we started a conversation. They were British and very proper, despite their attire. At close proximity, I realized that the light show I noticed between his legs was from the multiple piercings on his genitals — around a dozen barbells running from his ball sack up to the Prince Albert hanging from the tip of his cock. She also had rings sparkling from her labia.

This was not a scenario that you would normally see at a destination holiday resort: I knelt on the sidewalk looking up the skirts of a random couple as I investigated their exposed genital piercings. We talked with them for a while and realized they were a lovely couple who had found something they could share as a team while remaining true to themselves.

As we left them and walked back to our room, it was clear that they were there to remind us to not judge a book by its cover (or by looking up their skirt).

We met up with them the next day while waiting for our shuttle to the airport. They were heading to Hedonism II for another week of fun. When we commented on their seven large Louis Vuitton suitcases, they gave us a glimpse into our future of attending Lifestyle events. "It takes a lot of luggage to carry all the theme outfits and shoes for a week!" they said.

Hedonism III, was one of the most sexually liberating weeks Josh and I had ever experienced. After witnessing a multiplicity of sexual expressions and participating in many of them, we wanted more.

What the Hell Was That?

Each day that we were at Hedo III, our perspectives and attitudes changed. What seemed crazy one day became a fun activity the next. We were developing a MO that would continue to grow as we gained experiences, but our primary operative was to move toward pleasure, doing what felt right at the moment.

On our long flight back home from Jamaica, we had the opportunity to digest what had transpired over the week. We came to these discoveries:

• We liked checking in with each other to make sure that we were **RULE #1 MATES BEFORE DATES** comfortable and that we were on the same page. This became our Rule #1 - Mates Before Dates.

• We acknowledged that we both enjoyed our sexual experiences and watching our partner experience sexual pleasure. (We didn't know it then, but we were naturals at compersion.)

• We understood that typically woman would make the final decision **RULE #2 LADIES FIRST** on playing with others. That rule (learned from Nikki) became our Rule #2 - Ladies First.

• The feelings of jealousy were minimal and we addressed them through honest communication.

• The people who we connected with seemed like they were in solid relationships and deeply in love. We didn't witness any drama between them.

• Josh and I learned more about each other's sexuality and saw the positive changes that it was making in our relationship.

• It increased our libido and we both found the Lifestyle a huge turn-on. Not only were we having sex with other people, we were also having sex with each other more often. Our "reconnection" time after a play date became very important to us.

• In hindsight, we would decide whether a play date was a "Yes," a

"No," or a "Meh/Maybe." If something didn't feel right, we didn't do it again, but we always took that type of experience as some kind of a lesson.

Josh and I wanted more...more travel, more pleasure, more sex! This would be the next step in our evolution as a couple. And I got my wish to have more dicks!

Sexuality is one of the ways
that we become enlightened
actually, because it leads us
to self-knowledge.

- Alice Walker

Time to Play

The Lifestyle was expanding our mindset and cracking open our relationship. I was quickly realizing that it was a safe place for me to explore my sexuality. I could dress and act as sexy as I wanted to which was liberating. I enjoyed that even though I could expose parts of my body, I still had the authority to choose who could touch me.

Female Empowerment

During the first few play experiences we had at Hedonism, I embraced what my mentor had told me, "Women make the play decisions." This was different from the patriarchal society to which I was accustomed. I now had control of what, where and with whom I would share my body. It was a power that I was blessed to understand early on as it has served me well for many years in the Lifestyle. This is a major departure from the way I was brought up to behave.

I learned at a very young age to give away my power to others. I was told when to hug and kiss relatives or family friends, even when I didn't like their vibe. This practice overrode my gut feelings and tampered with my inner awareness. Like all children, I didn't have autonomy. Giving away my power was part of my programming: I was repressed at home, in church, and at school. By the age of eight, my mother had me walk back and forth in the living room with a book balanced on my head. Like a cross between a drill sergeant and a finishing school teacher, she would say, "Straight back, tuck in your bottom, suck in your stomach." She would repeat regularly, "Be a good girl, respect your elders, be a proper lady and only speak when spoken to." She wanted me to have a successful life and according to her manual, she was giving me instructions on how to do it.

I went through school as a shy little girl, hoping to fit in with the other kids. I was a follower, letting my friends make decisions for me. I laughed at their inappropriate jokes and got sucked up in the drama and rumors of others. As a girl, all of this was simply part of the social contract and I felt that I had to comply to survive.

By the time I entered the workforce at 16, I was groomed for following orders, all orders. Since I was the new girl on the office switchboard (yes, this is an old story), male department managers frequently engaged in conversation with me. There was one manager who consistently flirted with me, once even winking at me and grabbing his groin. I was disgusted by his actions but didn't know what to say or how to react.

That manager eventually asked me on a date. I felt strange about it because he was in his forties, almost a senior citizen from my perspective. I also felt obligated to go out with him because my parents always said, "Respect your elders and always be polite." Was it polite for me to say yes? It was confusing but I hadn't yet found my agency and my right to say no.

He arranged to pick me up outside the house because he knew he wouldn't be able to come to the door. I was a minor, after all, but fittingly over the age of legal consent. Once in the car, I remember him saying that he would drive around for a while, with no need for a restaurant. I politely agreed. I was nervous but sat there silently, reassuring myself that if I was polite, nothing bad would happen.

He parked the car and unzipped his pants, pulling out his cock. I had seen a couple of penises at parties when others were making out but never this close. I was shocked and terrified. He said, "You need to suck my penis. "What did he mean by "need"? He was my manager. Could he get me fired if I didn't do it? It wasn't a suggestion, it was a demand that I felt obligated to do. I was scared. It felt wrong but with no prior experience to sucking cock, I did as he instructed.

I felt like I had no control over what was happening to me as he pushed my head down multiple times onto his cock. It felt abnormal. Would that be what guys expected me to do? I was equally confused and ashamed. For self-preservation, I locked that experience deep in a vault within my mind.

Josh and I began dating not long after that incident. For over twenty years, blowjobs were something I did because it gave my partner pleasure. It was never about me. It took me decades before I remembered why. It was many years before I overcame that feeling of shame and lack of control over my life.

The "play nice with others" program was still deeply ingrained by the time that I married Josh. I felt that most of the decisions that we made were more Josh's ideas, but as we grew in our relationship, I began to speak up more with him and my other friends. That wasn't always easy because I needed those friends and saw the social value of being popular. Sometimes going along with what they said or did was the easy way.

At times, perhaps for balance, I would try aggression, but it never worked. I just sounded like a hormonal, bitchy woman. I know now that my aggression was my inexpert attempt to regain my power.

I guess what I really wanted was to feel listened to and understood. I wanted to express myself and have others listen to me without judgment. As I expressed my power in the Lifestyle, I grew stronger as a woman. This was one area that I could take control and feel good about myself. This was essential to my well-being. I could speak and respond truthfully to others, especially men. Most of the couples in the Lifestyle understood this way of thinking and acting. Women would talk and discuss how we would navigate a play session together. The men respected the women's choices and were delighted to engage in playtime. Josh especially knew how important it was for me to make these decisions.

Meeting my mentor when we first started in the Lifestyle was a game-changer. When she told me that women have all the power, it struck a chord that reverberated all the way to my sixteen year-old self and beyond.

My mind opened to the possibilities that were ahead of me and diverged from my experiences of the past. It was up to me to decide if I wanted to have oral sex with another man. Period. It would be on my terms. Period.

I would be in control. I could be as sexy as I wanted, and know that it would be my choice to engage in any kind of sex with another person. My body, my choice. It was empowering and deeply healing.

It was time to do the alchemy of turning what was once pain into... pleasure.

Who's on the Fuck Menu Tonight?

How did I choose the right guy to fuck? There were many criteria including:

1. He needed to be tall. I was like a carnival sign that says, "You must be this tall to ride." I stand nearly 6 feet in my stilettos, and I liked to look them straight in the eyes when we were vertical. This may have something to do with my father and brother being short. If the short men in my life had some complex against me because of my height, then maybe tall men would be different. Even when we were kids, Josh was one of the few boys my age taller than me and I found that attractive. I recall asking my early boyfriends to stand on a stair when we kissed so I didn't need to bend down. It didn't feel right. I was and still am, attracted to someone with height.

2. No facial hair, with a preference for men with less or no body hair. Definitely no fuzzy balls. Beards and mustaches were far too irritating and scratchy on my sensitive skin.

3. I've never been a size queen so the size of his dick didn't matter as long as he was average or above average. After giving birth to two children, I didn't have that tight little pussy I used to have in my 20s.

4. I also liked a guy with a great smile that showed their healthy teeth. Non-smokers were always preferred because I never liked kissing a dirty ashtray.

5. They needed to be good, sensual kissers. If they couldn't devote

any attention to foreplay, or be good at it, I just wasn't into it.

6. Last but definitely not least, I liked a physically fit man, well-dressed with a sense of their own style. Suits, jeans or board shorts didn't matter as long as they carried it well. My feelings were that if the guy expected me to present myself in my best way, then he should do the same and be a peacock. Equal opportunity.

Bonus points for... a sense of humor. I've always loved witty, intelligent men.

Once I scoped out the playing field and found a guy that visually checked off all the right boxes, I would check in with Josh to see if there was an attraction to the female of the couple. If there was, we would approach them and engage in conversation. If they seemed interesting, I would begin my flirting process. I would give the man my full attention by looking deeply into his eyes. Eye contact was and is very important to me. If their eyes wandered off to others in the room, then I knew I wouldn't be able to keep his attention in bed.

If a connection was there after a good discussion, the next step was to check out their lip service. A quick smooch on the lips would show him my interest. If there was a flutter in my stomach it was time to go deeper. I would allow my hands to gently explore his body and read his response to my touch. I could usually tell when they are too nervous, shy, inexperienced or too intoxicated.

Once that part of the interview was done, I would turn my attention back to the wife or partner. While Josh and the guy got to know each other, I would establish a relationship by chatting with her and finding a connection between us (fashion, makeup techniques, career choices, workout routines, travel destinations, or a random interest that we shared). I would always compliment her in some way, not manipulatively but because I enjoyed finding the thing that made someone sparkle. This would make her more relaxed and engaged and in turn, she would feel safe and sexy. Sometimes the attraction was deep and we would kiss each other; I love the feeling I get when kissing a woman. Josh would follow my lead and engage in conversation with the couple, looking to discover a four-way connection. He enjoyed watching me as the pursuer and he was also good at talking to the ladies. If everything looked tasty, it was time for room service or maybe just some heavy petting poolside.

I liked and desired control and knew what I wanted. I wanted to win the man's attention and their sexual favor. I wanted to succeed in attracting and fucking them. I wanted him to be another one of my sexual conquests. Instead of being a Womanizer....I was the Manizer, the one who pursued multiple casual relationships with men.

Josh - I have always loved watching Maggie on the prowl for new play-mates. She exudes confidence tempered with genuine warmth. Seeing her receive attention makes me appreciate her even more. She was a catch then and still is today.

I also fully grasp that this scenario isn't one-sided. I have experienced the situation where I am the man of interest being pursued by anoth-er woman. It doesn't matter to me whether I am a hunter or prey: Re-ceiving positive attention from the opposite sex is a boost to the ego and self-confidence.

It was playful game and we both enjoyed playing the game.

Mirror, Mirror on the Wall

Back in the early years, we were invited to a "Beautiful People's" Meet and Greet party. We had to be approved to go to the party and acceptance was solely based on how we looked. We knew one couple that the wife was approved but the husband was not. Josh and I weren't sure how we felt about it but, nonetheless, we decided to check it out.

The party could have been a beauty pageant — people posing everywhere and the focus remained solely on physical appearance. The party was clothing-optional, yet most people wore some kind of cover-up or bikini, some changing their bikinis several times during the night. The vibe was one of competition and comparison. There wasn't much merriment because, as Roosevelt was quoted to say, "Comparison is the thief of joy."

It was those kinds of parties that would bring out all sorts of anxieties about my body. I may have been an adult, but part of me was still the heavy, stout 9 year old girl. As mentioned, I was taller than my older brother who teased me, probably feeling weird about his younger sister being taller than him.

I was happiest when I was eating. It was one of life's pleasures that didn't seem to be classified as a sin. Food was my comfort, but my dad would always stop me from going back for seconds. He would remind me that if I ate too much I would be a *butchka* (Ukrainian word for Barrel). This started my interesting relationship with food and body image.

At 9 years old, I noticed my mother on diets, tracking her weight daily. She encouraged me to do the same so even as a growing kid, I would weigh myself every day, hoping to drop a pound or two. The diets were an annual thing my mother and I would do together. Female bonding. By the time I turned 12 and puberty hit, all my weight came off and I grew another 3 inches.

As a teenager, I still retained my childhood insecurity and shyness. I was 5'8" tall, 120 pounds, with AA breasts. My body was kinda boyish— straight with no hips. This made me self-conscious and I felt uncomfortable in my clothes. At 22, I had a breast enlargement procedure that helped me deal with my insecurities. I embraced my new perfect B's and they boosted my confidence.

Fast forward a decade and two kids later...my weight changed and my addiction to diets and daily weigh-ins returned. I wasn't overweight, but I wasn't secure in my own skin. I thought that losing weight would make others find me more attractive and desirable. That was something I battled for the next 20 years.

After breastfeeding two babies, it was time to have my implants replaced. I wanted to go bigger so I increased to a C cup. I loved my new set and was proud to show them off. I bought lots of tight-fitting clothing and seductive lingerie. I felt and looked sexy, even to myself.

Let's face it, by choosing the Lifestyle, I was choosing to disrobe in front of many people and this was bound to bring up body image insecurities. I dealt with those by doing mirror work. I made a practice of standing naked in the mirror and noting all the beautiful parts of my body and face. I had no problem commenting on other women's beauty; it was time that my gaze went to my own beauty instead of my perceived imperfections. I would tell myself how hot and sexy I

was, and as time went on, I started believing it. I consciously projected a positive, energetic, sexy and playful vibe. I would reassure Josh
too, by expressing how sexy and desirable he was and how his body
turned me on. This was just as important for him to hear as well.

We've met people of all sizes and shapes in the Lifestyle. I recall
one larger woman who wore tight-fitting, sexy dresses with a push-
up bra and come-fuck-me shoes. She was voluptuous and she knew
how to work it. She owned it and I could feel her self-confidence oozing from her. I admired her positive, sexy, energy and often thought
of her for inspiration.

I had changed how I looked on the outside, but I still had work to do
with how I felt on the inside. This work would take time.

Keeping it Local

After our Hedo Swinger "cherry poppin," Josh and I were looking to
maintain that level of excitement and play style. We found that our
overall happiness increased and that was reason enough to find a local Swinger community. Our yearly adult trips weren't enough fulfillment for us so we began to attend local events and meet new friends
who shared our interests. We were introduced to our first Lifestyle
focused websites and it was opening up a world of opportunities,
both locally and internationally.

Locally, one of the couples we met was Ken and Brianna, Lifestyle
event organizers. They would rent restaurants and bars to provide a
venue for Swinger "Meet and Greets." Those events were never SOP
(Sex on Premises) but they were a great opportunity to flirt and get
to know other couples. We would often get invited to an after-party at someone's home or hotel suite and satisfy the built-up sexual
cravings.

I was thrilled to be a part of the local scene which allowed me to
make personal connections with other pleasure-seeking women. It
was different from the PTA meetings which bored me with discussions of kids, politics and the weather. When pleasure-seeking wom-
en got together, there was a stream of ideas and tips that were titillating and sexually arousing. On one occasion, an exotic dancer saw me

struggling with my sexy outfit while in the bathroom and shared her secret of wearing her g-string on the outside of her garter belt. This costume modification made playtime much simpler. Easy access.

My newfound Sorority of Swingers was deeply satisfying, on many levels. We would share our playlists of sexy erotic music, talk about our favorite sex toys, or tell which spas offered good deals on Botox and Fillers. At that time, facial rejuvenation was part of my method to attract multiple partners. With peacocks, it's the males with the showy plumage; with Swingers, it was and is the females. Yes, the women made the decisions but we were also the ones on display. It was just "good marketing" as Josh used to say.

Underlying all the female interactions was a code of conduct which

RULE #3 DON'T KISS & TELL became our Rule Number 3 - Don't Kiss and Tell. Once we would become intimate with another couple, the conversations became very personal and private. We were there for pleasure so sharing drama or creating drama through gossip was out of the question. What happened with Swingers, stayed … in the bedroom.

Our community grew as we consensually introduced our favorite couples to other Lifestylers and vice versa. It was like online dating with someone else "swiping right" for us. We were getting enthusiastic "two thumbs up" approvals from our play partners. Life was good. As we met more people, we were invited to more parties, some of which were in our own neighborhood.

Seeing the demand for more venues, one couple converted their home into an adult playhouse complete with a dance floor, stripper pole, a bar, play spaces, and a kinky play area. They held semimonthly parties and offered a small changing room for those who needed to transform when they arrived. When our kids lived at home, I would cover my sexy attire with a long trench coat. I couldn't be both the Madonna and the Whore, could I? And even if I could, my young sons sure didn't want to know about it.

F*cking Our Way to Enlightenment

Josh - Maggie and I were invited to the adult play house for a To-ga-themed party. It was a full house and there were plenty of people who caught our attention. I was standing alone near the dance floor when Sandi introduced herself to me and began a conversation. The music was loud and to be heard, we had to lean in and talk into each other's ear. From such close proximity, I could feel the strong attraction between the two of us.

Maggie was off chatting at the bar so I asked Sandi to dance. As we ground to the beats, I noticed her white robe as it draped over her breasts. Her erect nipples pushed and rubbed against me. Her confidence reminded me of Maggie and as I looked into her eyes, I sensed her desire.

The music guided our movements as we kissed and fondled each other's bodies. Slowly and teasingly, Sandi dropped down to her knees and lifted up my toga, exposing my semi-erect cock. I've never considered myself an exhibitionist but the approving and envious glances from the others on the dance floor added fuel to my own fire. My cock continued to grow as Sandi's eyes remained fixed on mine. Her lips teased my tip, flicking her tongue back and forth, coaxing it to attention.

I was enjoying our PDA and was admittedly proud that I could rise to the occasion. She wetly licked and sucked my shaft as I stood there, fully receiving her attention and feeling it amplified by the crowded dance floor. An exhibitionist is defined as someone who acts in an extravagant way in order to get attention. That wasn't what I was doing. I was in the moment, and what I was doing was getting attention and I could feel that attention feeding our desire.

I wanted to fuck her so badly. We left the dance floor in search of Maggie and Sandi's partner. We found them in the bar area and after some conversation, we/I suggested that we take this party upstairs to one of the playrooms. I was pleased that they both agreed.

The parties we attended in our city were fun but they lacked the BIG party feel with costumes, entertainment and exotic locations. Those destination holidays allowed us to live fully without the confines of our home life. A few of our new friends were going to a party in Vegas and it sounded like it was going to be epic. The timing was right so we booked the trip.

The Bathroom Shower

One of the grand Vegas hotels hosted an epic Lifestyles Convention with a few thousand people of all shapes, sizes and ages. It wasn't a complete hotel takeover so several precautions were in place to keep the Swingers and non-Swingers (or Vanillas) from too much exposure to each other. The swimming pool had a high privacy fence installed to keep the gawkers at bay and there were rules for how much skin could be exposed in the common areas. It became a challenge to see what I could get away with before catching the watchful eyes of the security guards (who seemed happy to police the event).

The huge convention rooms were decorated and the live entertainment kept the dance floor filled. The attendees ranged from young porn starlets to seniors - one of whom was pushing his walker and oxygen tank. At first, I was a little shocked but then I gave the guy props for still going at it. The invention of Viagra has made 80 the new 40.

A few of our fellow Canadians secured penthouse suites at either end of the hotel. This became the "Canadian Double Ender" party with each suite having a different ambience: One was dimly lit with sexy chill tunes playing, and the other was upbeat with a couple of oil-filled kiddy pools in the living room.

After starting the evening in the chill suite, Josh and I walked over to the other party which was in full swing, which is Swinger code for a wild orgy. The doorman greeted us by asking us to take off our tops, down to the skin, an immediate ice-breaker. As we looked around, we saw around 80 people having sex in every way imaginable. Everywhere we turned...people were fucking, sucking, or licking. They were on the sofas, chairs, beds and floor. Some leaned against the large picture windows and were getting fucked from behind. The cries of pleasure creating a sexual symphony of sound. The momentary wallflowers watched or chatted, savoring the view on both sides of the window.

Close to the door, a very attractive couple remained unengaged to the action. They looked like the perfect all-American couple so we'll call them Barbie and Ken. I turned to Josh and signalled my interest.

We walked toward them, weaving through the naked bodies. We introduced ourselves and began a flirtatious conversation. After a short while, I asked Ken if he had ever received an Altoid mint blowjob. He said no, but said that he would love to receive one. I popped an Altoid in my mouth and we navigated the room in search of a space to make out.

Meanwhile, Barbie and Josh wandered amongst the naked bodies on their own quest for some horizontal real estate. They found some stuck between a king sized bed and a wall. Not the most comfortable, but at least it was space.

The combined sexual energy in the penthouse suite was intense. It was turning me on big time. I wanted to be close to Josh but there was no room on the floor next to him. I looked around and noticed a beautiful open-style bathroom.

Ken and I found a small plot in the walk-in shower. We ripped off our remaining clothes (except my signature stilettos) and we kissed each other intensely. Then, I got to work. The tingling sensation of the mint on his penis excited him and he was quickly close to coming. I slowed things down and he asked, "Would you like your pussy licked?" Yes please, was almost always the answer.

Our first configuration involved the tile floor but it was cold and uncomfortable, so Ken suggested we move. Real estate being scarce, I sat on the toilet tank while he fingered me. I always enjoyed new ways to lose my virginity, and toilet sex was a first.

I leaned back against the wall as he slowly slid his two fingers into my wet opening. I added my moans to the orgy cacophony as his fingers went in and out of me. I knew I was close to coming but I really wanted to squirt so I expressed my desire. Ken replied with a smile and a change in fingering technique.

One of our washroom neighbors overheard our conversation; she asked me if she could put her head between my legs and catch my juices when I came. Why would I say no?

I stabilized myself as I leaned against the tank, straddling the toilet. The young hottie sat down on the floor and leaned her head back on the toilet seat, looking up at me. Ken put his two fingers inside my impatient pussy and began to massage my G-spot. I guided him,

"Harder, harder. Faster, faster."

He pumped his fingers until I exploded. My shower drenched the waiting goddess beneath me. I was spent, Ken was thrilled, and our new friend beneath me was satisfied. We had found a way to turn cheap real estate into a memorable evening.

Lady in White

As the convention continued, I made my way through my sexy themed costumes. The one that got me into the most trouble, (if you could call it that) was the naughty angel costume. I had full white feather wings, a furry halo, bare legs topped with white thigh-high come-fuck-me boots, a white lacy demi-cup bra and matching boy shorts. I topped it off with a long platinum blonde wig with flowing white ribbons that cascaded over my breasts. I looked hot and felt confident as Josh and I headed off to the White Party.

When we got there we found 3000 Lifestylers busy working the room, looking for the next play partner or stimulating conversation. The room was loud with excitement and lust. The opportunities seemed endless but that didn't automatically mean more sex. It was difficult to keep track of everyone we met and our conversations were often disjointed because of all the distractions. It was more quantity over quality but that wasn't going to stop us from having a good time.

About mid-way through the evening the MC announced that there would be a Sexy Costume Contest. Josh and several others encouraged me to enter so I took their prodding and gathered my courage. I strutted up to the stage in my white 6-inch platform boots, feeling excited yet nervous. The DJ played as we each took the spotlight and performed our solo seductive dance. I shook my hips, jiggled my breasts and sashayed all the way to the finals. As I stood in the spotlight, I felt powerful and beautiful. I could be as wild as I wanted to be and I felt free. I knew who I was and although the judges placed me as runner-up, my newfound confidence felt like a win.

Later that night, Josh and I were invited to a private after-party at Siegfried & Roy's old house in the suburbs of Vegas. The middle of the living room featured an immense windowed cage that the infamous magicians would use to view their white tigers. For the Swinger event, the party planners filled the cage with fuzzy white blankets and pillows, converting it into an inviting playroom. Out with the old pussy, in with the new.

My white ensemble matched the environment perfectly. As I looked over to my right, I spotted a stunning woman, Abby, also dressed in white. She stood there with only a bustier, white thong, and stiletto heels. I turned into a white tigress as I stared at her alluring movements and sexy smile. When she met my eyes with her intense gaze, I knew it was "game on."

I invited Abby into the tiger's den and she excitedly agreed. She crawled into the cage heading toward the furry white bed and pulled me in to join her. We moved closer as we crawled around like two cats in heat. As I stared into her bright blue eyes, I could sense people gathering to watch us perform. I crawled in closer and breathed down her neck. My warm breath aroused her and her breathing became audible. I gently nibbled on her ears and she moaned with pleasure. I felt warm desire wash over me as my tongue entered her mouth. I slid my hand under her bustier and squeezed her breast. Her skin was so soft and her perky flesh fit perfectly in my hand.

It was Abby's turn to be the predator. She pulled at my bra, releasing my breasts. I let out a moan and threw back my head, enjoying the erotic moment. My nipples became sensitized, yearning for her attention. Sensing my desire, she placed her full lips on them. I groaned with satisfaction.

Feeling the sexual charge between us amplifying, we embraced each other, pressing our soft breasts together. We kissed wildly as the aroused onlookers observed through the glass. I realized then how much I enjoyed being with another woman. Being an exhibitionist added to my turn-on but I figured that if we were going to go any further, we needed to find some privacy. The guest house was open and we made a break for it. It was there that we created a sexy bit of heaven.

The Lust Boat

2400 Swingers, cruising for action from Florida to the Mexican Riviera. What's not to lust? Josh and I made contact with several couples on the host's website forum and were excited to meet them in the flesh.

The Meet and Greet was held at a local nightclub. We were hungry lions on the prowl, excited for who would be our next prey. The sexual energy was cranked and nobody even thought about sleep until the wee hours of the morning.

When we boarded the next day, the boat became an immense city of Swingers. It was like a giant, sexy smorgasbord with people of every size and shape. One waiter noted that he had never heard the ship's dining area so loud with conversation. Instead of older married couples staring silently at their food, passengers were moving between tables, flirting ferociously.

The ship had a policy that if you wanted to drink, you had to buy one of the over-priced drink packages. That set up a challenge to see who, from our new tribe of friends, could smuggle booze on board. It wasn't that we couldn't afford the package, we just didn't like being told what to do and how to do it. It brought out the rebel in all of us.

I had pre-emptively ordered a Winerack - a clear vinyl bra that was capable of holding a full 26-ounce bottle of alcohol. Genius. Within a couple of days we stopped in Cozumel and took the opportunity to replenish the bra. We walked into town with a bunch of new friends, flirting with each other easily, and enjoying our chosen Lifestyle. We found a liquor store and bought a "two-sixer" of vodka. In the exhibitionist style that we were slowly adopting, we decided to stand on the public sidewalk to fill the Winerack, allowing the locals to catch glimpses of my breasts. When the rack was replenished, it was time to head back to the ship.

It was a scorching hot day which is why I didn't immediately notice that my right breast was leaking vodka. The constant drip-drip from my nipple region turned my white t-shirt into a wet t-shirt but thankfully with the heat, the vodka was evaporating quickly. We were all laughing as we approached the ship's checkpoint and I hoped I wasn't attracting too much attention. Fortunately they must have thought I just needed to get home to breastfeed so they waved me through security. Thankfully, vodka has no odor.

The Lust Boat was a great combination of our favorite things: like-minded people, fun, sex, and travel. It was exciting and new and just like the theme song from that old sitcom, it "promised something for everyone." We knew that we would soon be making another run.

The Watcher

When it was time to take a break from our everyday life, we decided to head back to Jamaica, but this time we would brave Hedo II. At that point, we had been seasoned and were ready for something spicier.

The resort didn't disappoint. One afternoon I noticed a young stud peeping through the chain link fence that segregated the Hedo property from the adjacent family-friendly one. He couldn't resist checking out the nudies-next-door and his curiosity gave me an idea...

The openness that Josh and I had developed allowed me to freely express my fantasies. I told him that I wanted to re-enact a scene from the movie "True Lies." I envisioned Josh sitting in the corner of our hotel suite with the lights off as he watched me perform a sexy dance on the bed, but in my rendition, Josh would be cuckolded. The thought of it aroused both Josh and myself, all we needed was the stud.

I got the peeping stud's attention by wearing a black cover-up that thinly veiled my large dark nipples and curves. I strutted over to the young man, whose name was Chad, and introduced myself. He was a hot, surfer dude, completely opposite to Josh. I tested the waters to see if Chad was interested in me. He was in, and we arranged the details of smuggling him into our resort.

After dinner, Josh and I danced in the nightclub, steeping ourselves in the sexy vibes. At 10 pm, I walked into the lobby and met up with Chad to escort my new playmate back to the club. Weaving through the dance floor packed with semi-naked bodies, we found a spot to dance. Chad was in his personal heaven surrounded by the sexiness that he was only drooling at a few hours before.

We hadn't danced long before I whispered in Josh's ear, "Could you go to the suite and set the mood for our playtime?" I wanted him to sit naked in the corner and watch me fuck this young stud. Josh willingly agreed.

When I led Chad up to our suite, I informed him that my husband was going to be in the room and that he would be watching us. I sensed his nervousness as we approached the door. I relaxed him by explaining that it was completely consensual and desired by all participants.

We entered the room and as I requested, Josh was sitting naked in the corner of the suite. The anticipation alone was arousing me: I would be a "top" for that hour and I was going to perform for Josh. I was making the orders and they were along for the ride.

The lights were turned low to maintain the clandestine feel. Chad sat on the bed and surrendered to my moves. I pulled off his clothes and then slowly and sexually unbuttoned mine. The garments dropped to my feet and revealed my naked curves.

I moved to the bed and Chad kissed my neck then progressed to my lips, kissing me deeply with his hungry tongue. My breasts were his next target and he teased my nipples with little nibbles and licks. As I reclined on the bed, I looked over at Josh who was stroking himself, thoroughly enjoying the show.

I instructed my new boy toy to put his hands between my legs and touch me. As his fingers brushed against my inner thigh, I opened my legs wide. I suggested that he kiss and lick me gently. He didn't seem sure of his techniques, so I provided helpful instructions on how to suck on my clit and slide two fingers into my pussy. You're welcome, all of Chad's future lovers.

I opened up even wider as his fingers parted my folds and caressed my clit. I let out a shiver as I felt a rush of pleasure. My wetness was flowing as he pushed his fingers deeper inside of me, slowly finger fucking me. I moaned and heard Josh's groans of approval from the corner. I knew my beloved was excited to watch me enjoy myself yet I sensed Chad was feeling uncomfortable with my hubby present.

I reassured him again that Josh was enjoying every moment of our playtime.

Chad's apprehension did nothing to deter his raging hard on. I took his cock in one hand and caressed his balls with my other. As I stroked and kissed it, I sensed that he was close to coming so I mounted him, rubbing my wet pussy on his big, juicy balls. I ground my hips and dangled my boobs in front of his face. My nipple fell easily into his mouth and he sucked it gently, making my pussy ache for him.

My eyes locked on his as I reached over for a condom on the bedside table. (Rule number 4 - Practice safe sex) I slipped on the rubber and straddled him, feeling the tip of his cock slide past my labia into my wet, warm depths. The pleasure was intense as his penis stretched me out. When I was ready to come, I used my fingers to rub my juicy clit. I thrust my hips and ground against his strong, toned body. The feeling of his cock inside of me, my control, and Josh being cuckolded was bringing me to an orgasmic body high. I moaned with ecstasy, my whole body tingling. I clutched my breasts as Chad and I both came. From the corner, Josh's orgasm was a few strokes away. I watched with enjoyment as he pushed himself over the edge.

RULE #4 PRACTICE SAFE SEX

Josh joined us on the bed, kissing me passionately, Chad's cock still glistening with my juices. I was sandwiched between two men with layers of pleasure, control, and satisfaction.

After a bit of small talk, we dressed. I escorted Chad back to the lobby and kissed him goodbye, thanking him for the memorable night. If he ever tried sharing his locker room story to reluctant believers, this book is proof that it happened, unfortunately under an alias.

After that night, Josh and I encouraged each other to explore more sexual fantasies. Our playtimes became filled with, "What else is possible?"

The World Wide Web... of Swingers

With the expansion of the Internet, it became much easier to find people with similar kinks and desires. Interest in the Lifestyle was growing quickly with more clubs and events emerging around the globe. During our first ten years, the number of active participants grew exponentially. It was also easier for organizers to facilitate large hotel and resort takeovers.

Luxury Lifestyle Vacations had an offer that interested us enough to book a beachside room. They had reserved an entire all-inclusive resort near Cabo San Lucas for a week-long Swinger party. The main ballroom was converted into a nightclub and a playroom was set up in another smaller event room. Each night, the decorations coincided with the evening's party theme. They brought in dance poles and cages along with world-class DJs, stage effects and lighting. The playroom was set up with beds, sensual decor and soft, mood lighting. It was a convention room filled with beds, the perfect place for both exhibitionists and voyeurs.

During the day, the room was used for workshops and seminars. There was one workshop that we will never forget...

The Blowjob Master Class

After lunch one afternoon, Josh and I entered a crowded convention room to learn the Art of Blowing. The mattresses in the room had been stacked in layers so they were well placed for the techniques we were about to learn. A female instructor knelt on a riser with her naked stud sitting before her.

The 30 couples took their positions with the men naked and sitting on the edge of the beds as the women knelt before them. It was surreal to witness and participate in a semi-naked workshop — part business, part pleasure. School had never been so fun! After a little introduction and an anatomy lesson, our instructor demonstrated her oral pleasuring skills.

Josh - Just as the class was beginning, Maggie, who was kneeling in front of me, began talking to the attractive blonde next to her. Moments later they swapped positions and Jenny had repositioned herself at my feet, raising her arm to shake my hand. Her husband Mike, who was sitting beside me, greeted me as his wife familiarized herself with my equipment.

The instructor explained a few new-to-us techniques, one of which involved a deep throat technique. Maggie never did that with me (at that time, neither of us knew why). It was a new sensation that I secretly hoped she would enjoy. The mood was both fun and erotic. There were giggles, moans of ecstasy, and the occasional gag when someone went a bit too deep.

It was surreal to be in a room full of naked men, receiving oral sex from a woman whom I had only met moments before. The combination of sensory stimulation, the sounds of sex, the visuals of watching others, and the oral attention that I was receiving was intensely enjoyable!

The event came to a close with a happy ending for our instructor and her collaborator. Maggie, always filled with good ideas, invited Jenny and Mike to join us down at the pool. I expanded her offer and asked if they would like to join us in our room. They quickly agreed and as we left, we picked up another couple whom they knew, to join us in our room. The six of us went back to our suite and the girls were rewarded with their own tongue-lashing and more.

From that chance encounter, we have become good friends with Jenny and Mike. We've traveled the globe together and we continue to experience new adventures.

My adventures with Josh were always filled with pleasure but sometimes, tucked inside, was also a lesson. And a new rule...

Taking One for the Team

Chloe was a beautiful and sensual woman whom we had met on our first trip to Desire. She had caught Josh's eye earlier in the day and he gave me the "look" which meant he was interested in meeting her. When we saw her by the pool later, we took the opportunity to introduce ourselves. She was by herself and welcomed our company so we suntanned by the pool most of the afternoon while getting to know each other.

There seemed to be a connection so Josh asked me if I would like some playtime with her. Immediately, I agreed and asked Chloe if she would be interested. She said absolutely, but she and her husband always played as a couple. We agreed thinking that if we had a connection with her, we would also have one with her husband. We were wrong.

When Jorge arrived on the scene, he and I had zero connection: There was no spark, no tingle in my pussy, not even a slight attraction to him physically. But Josh was so smitten by Chloe, and I so wanted to facilitate his desire.

The four of us went back to their room. Chloe boarded Josh's beef bus without much time waiting at the station. Jorge and I didn't have such luck. We moved over to the couch, waiting for something to happen. I could feel his hesitation — maybe the feeling was mutual or maybe he could feel my vibe. We tried kissing to see if it would spark something, I even asked him to kiss my pussy, but nothing worked. Nada. Not a thing. Crickets.

I glanced over at Josh, hoping he would notice how uncomfortable I was, but his full attention was on Chloe. And why not? She was so stunning that I found myself attracted to her. At least I got to watch my husband starring in live porn.

At one point, Josh noticed that things weren't connecting on my end so he and Chloe turned their attention to us. We awkwardly joined them on the bed as the playtime slowed to a crawl.

But I was angry. When I looked for someone to be angry at, I couldn't blame anyone but myself. If I was in charge of arranging the playdate, I was also to blame for allowing the encounter to go that way. If I was in control of the decisions, it was my job to create situations that I would enjoy. That was the first, and last time that I ever took one for the team. It was a good lesson that led to another rule: Rule #6 - Always connect with all partners before agreeing to a hook-up.

Even Desire has Limits

Josh and I never had hard-and-fast rules for our playtime sessions, although along the way (through experience and mistakes) we created a few guidelines that we found useful. We've called them rules but they're really a guide to playing well with others. Our main MO has always been allowing the play time to flow, moving towards what we enjoy and away from what we don't. It was that first trip to Desire that I pushed the boundaries of our playtime.

As mentioned, I wanted to be the dominant one in all my encounters with other men. I would be the one to initiate the playtime and I would usually tell them when to lick my pussy, when to fondle my breasts or when to stick their hard cock into me. As a response to my earlier trauma, I would need to be the top, controlling their penis and making sure that I was satisfied first. When I felt the desire to fuck someone, I was in control.

One night on the dance floor, I decided to exercise this control with my hot dancing partner. I leaned over to him and asked if he would like to have a quickie with me. I don't recall asking what the rules he had with his partner were, I just craved a power trip. He immediately agreed so I took his hand and led him off to the men's restroom.

Josh had no idea where I was, but part of me wanted to see if Josh would care enough to say something. Well, he did.

 This is Rule number 6 - Always meet each other's potential play partners...Before! Josh expressed how scared and concerned he was for me. He said I should always let him meet the guy, just to make sure that this stranger respected me and our relationship. Strangely, I was glad he requested that I never do it again. I realized how much he cared for me and how much he wanted to make sure I was safe. It wasn't a trust issue between Josh and me, but a safety concern.

Josh - There have only been a few times that I have had any negative feelings about the Lifestyle. They have mostly been caused by other men not respecting our partnership. I have had men step between Maggie and me, and show me their backs, something that is deeply disrespectful. I understand that there is a long history of competition between men for the attention of females, but it's time we all change.

Single men are more prone to this behavior but we have seen it in married men as well. Trust me, it won't get you very far, at least not with us. Ask permission, acknowledge the husband, and show me why I should trust you with my wife.

The first time I felt any negative emotions about our Lifestyle was when we were at an event in Mexico. It was one of our first hotel takeover events. We were in the resort's nightclub and Maggie left with a guy that I had not met. I didn't know where they were and it bothered me, not that she was off fucking some guy, but because I didn't meet him first or know his story. I want to feel his intention and look him in the eye. I was concerned for her safety and wanted her to have an enjoyable time.

We learned something that night and since then we have always made sure there was a connection between all of us before wandering off.

Squirting 101

Squirting had become a "thing" in the Lifestyle scene...part orgasm and part show for some women. I was intrigued.

The LLV organizers at Desire had arranged a few workshops, and one was on squirting. The facilitators set up a bed in the middle of the dance floor and about 50 of us gathered around to see the demo. This included a female anatomy simulator that used a turkey baster and rubber ring to create a simple representation of the body parts involved. It didn't look like any body parts we are familiar with but it helped with the demonstration.

The instructor had his wife lift her beach wrap and lay on the bed, knees up and spread. There was no foreplay or checking in with her. After a short description of the technique, he casually slipped his two middle fingers into her waiting pussy and began fiercely slamming them in and out, to sounds of loud splishing and sploshing. Within seconds, she began to squirt profusely and it was over almost as quickly as it started. Josh and I found the whole presentation a bit absurd but it did encourage us to go back to our room and see how big of a wet spot I could make.

We met a young couple, Shania and Steve, at another "Learn To Squirt" demonstration. They were new to open relationships and were eager to learn so it was time for us to step into the mentor role.

After the workshop, we all went back to their stateroom on the ship, for some grounding and pounding. Once round one was done, we lay together with our hair freshly fucked. Through our casual conversation, they found out that I was an experienced squirter. Shania asked me to show her husband, Steve, how to make her squirt. I thought it would be best if I demonstrated while she watched. She loved the idea so I got to work. I picked up a couple of large towels and placed them on the bed. I asked Steve to kneel beside me and I did the same as we faced each other. I instructed him to put his middle and ring finger inside my still-wet pussy. He smiled from ear to ear, willingly following my commands. I asked him to press his fingers firmly along the inner front wall of the vagina and to begin stroking in a downward motion, milking the Grafenberg spot (G-spot). I could feel the pressure building inside of me. I knew I was engorged and I could feel the gland inside my pussy, ready to explode. I said, "Harder, harder, faster, faster." Our audience watched with anticipation as they sat on the bed.

Steve moved his fingers faster and pressed harder against the inner gland. I ordered him to continue stroking and with a shriek of satisfaction, I released a human fountain on the towel. I looked over at wide-eyed Shania as she squealed with excitement. Then I glanced at Josh and noticed how thrilled he was to see her reaction. It was rewarding to step into the role of the teacher, as many others had done for us.

Let's Go Cruisin' in Europe

Josh and I had found our happy place so it didn't take much to convince us to join some of our new friends on another cruise. Our favorite tour organizers had booked an entire cruise ship for a trip along the Adriatic coast from Venice to Dubrovnik. It was an ideally sized ship that held about 700 guests and featured 5-star service.

We decided to spend some time connecting prior to the cruise so we made a romantic stop in Paris, observing our Rule #1 - Mates Before Dates. After a couple of days in the City of Lights, we took an overnight train to Venice and boarded the ship.

This trip hooked us into the Lifestyle cruise world. The organizers chose some great themes for the nightly parties. The DJs spun all day for the pool crowd as extra musicians and dancers performed. The pool and above deck areas were clothing optional except when the ship was in port. There were always the rebels who paraded naked, despite the rules.

The organizers cleared out one of the main dining rooms to create a spacious playroom. Panoramic windows gave a view of the stern of the ship and a sea of beds covered the floors. We were Swingers — prime real estate was for fucking, not eating. I thought about the cruisers who were going to be sitting around a quiet table enjoying their meals, not realizing that hundreds of people were sport fucking in that exact spot a week earlier.

One afternoon when we were cruising, Josh and I retreated to our room for some alone time. As we stood on the balcony overlooking the sea and distant landforms, Josh began to remove what little clothing I had on. Bending me over the balcony, he slipped a couple fingers into my pussy, preparing it for his cock. I was ready for it, and he knew it. It was really hot getting slammed from behind as the bright sun toasted our naked bodies.

The sounds of arousal must have caught our upstairs neighbor's attention. Slowly, a Lelo vibrator attached to a long ribbon was dangled down from the suite above us. I released it with amusement and we went back inside and did a little product testing on my pussy. It worked extremely well so we wrote a thank-you note, attached it to the clean vibe, tied it back to the ribbon and left it hanging there for them to retrieve. We liked that about many Lifestyle couples, always there to lend a playful helping hand (or vibe).

The smaller ship was definitely better for us; it was big enough to have all the luxury and facilities but small enough that we didn't lose each other in the expanse. Being on a boat, exploring the world and our bodies with like-minded people was addictive, at least to us. There were many facets that made it pleasurable: Novelty, the hormonal rushes, the continued expansion of our sexual repertoire, being surrounded by beauty...the list continued. Josh and I had created a life of never knowing what adventure was around the corner. We loved it.

Another Trip to Pleasure City

Our next trip to Vegas was for another full takeover party but this time it was at a small resort just off the strip. There were a couple of hundred people and it was just a few days long. It struck us as odd that Sin City did not allow any nudity even in an enclosed resort takeover. The girls pushed those rules pretty far with the tiniest string bikinis and nipple pasties.

While we were there, a few Canadians had reserved a poolside cabana and Josh and I were invited to join them. One of them had temporary maple leaf tattoos that read "Canadians, just do 'em," a nod to the popular Nike slogan. The tats were a great icebreaker and soon many boobs and bums were decorated with the red maple leaf tattoo.

Space in the resort was limited. One night they offered a field trip to a large casino nightclub that was hosting a Pimp 'n Ho theme party. The organizers had arranged large, limo-type buses to shuttle us between the venues. Hundreds of men in iconic velvet suits, wide-brim hats, and dangling bling escorted women with busting boobs wearing sky-high stilettos and boots, minuscule skirts, and fishnet stockings. As we paraded by the casino, we were quite a distraction for the patrons who lost interest in their slots.

That night brought our attention to the drinking and drug habits of some of those around us. It was beginning to be a bit too much party for us, we couldn't stay awake that late. Alcohol was useful to help loosen inhibitions, but it also decreased the sensations for many guys leading to underwhelming erections. We also noticed that cocaine and ecstasy were invading the parties. Both had side effects that can dampened the play.

I also relied on the booze to surrender my inhibitions and ease my nerves. Josh hadn't realized the anxiety that I faced - the childhood programming around female sexuality and cultural norms had embedded certain beliefs in me that I needed to dull for me to enjoy my pleasure.

We were invited to more than a few play parties that became too much coke and not enough poke. We tried to avoid those and would excuse ourselves if it was headed in that direction. But sometimes, we had to excuse ourselves for other reasons...

The Captain's Hook

Our informal "Meet and Greets" were always by the pool. We could get a good sense of people and we could check out their bodies. Our previous playmates would also introduce us to their favorite playmates. It was a social endorsement and just good sharing.

This was not different during our visit to Hedo II when I was introduced to a man twenty years older than me. He was called "The Captain." He had a certain swagger, strutting around the resort with two or even three women on his arm (in a kind of chain). He was loud and crass and enjoyed being the center of attention. I didn't get a good vibe from him when we were introduced. He seemed sleazy and aggressive.

Later that afternoon we were invited to a small orgy: Five couples including us were there to play. Josh and I knew everyone and felt comfortable with them so when we arrived at the suite, we almost immediately piled on the king size bed and the couch. With everyone licking, sucking and kissing body parts feverishly, it was like interactive porn.

A few minutes later, The Captain stormed the room and gracelessly pounced on the bed. His groping eyes soon found me and he lumbered my way. Not wanting to disrupt play, I quickly moved to the far side of the bed. I eased into Josh's scene and kissed the woman whose pussy he had in his mouth. This did nothing to deter the Captain's gaze. My heart raced as he moved towards me again. It was a cat-and-mouse game and I was the unwilling prey.

Quickly, I repositioned myself on the couch and asked if I could jump into another couple's scene. They agreed but as I looked over at The Captain, he mouthed the words, "I'm coming for you." I didn't enjoy his game — he was not following consent protocol by asking before advancing on a woman. I glanced at Josh, but he was so deep in a pussy, he didn't notice. Again, I saw the lust in The Captain's eyes as he licked his lips and mouthed, "I want you." Ewwww, I was sixteen again, grossed out and a little scared.

I got up from the couch and tapped Josh on the shoulder and said, "I need to talk to you, now." He followed me into the bathroom and we closed the door. I explained that The Captain was grossing me out. I was not interested in him touching me in any way. I suggested that we leave immediately.

Josh was so understanding. Without a second thought, he said, "Ok, let's go." (This is Mates before Dates in action.) So we gathered our clothes and said a quick goodbye.

Life is like a spiral. The lessons that we learn come around again so that we can choose another outcome. The Captain was my boss: His energy was similar, he was my elder, and he was lewd and loud. I, however, was twenty-five years older the second time. I had finally found my "No."

Don't be afraid.
Don't be ashamed.
Don't ever apologize
for your sexuality.
Just be you.

- Sonya Deville

F*cking Our Way to Enlightenment

Where Do We Go From Here?

Josh and I have the ability to go from Michelin-starred restaurants to truck stop diners, engaging with the people around us wherever we land. We enjoy a wide variety of experiences and we also enjoy sharing them with our Lifestyle friends.

Sturgis is one of the premier motorcycle rallies in the USA. Held annually, it attracts well over 500,000 bikers to South Dakota. The first time attending the rally we rented a large RV and towed a trailer with our Harley. The RV was both our accommodation and closet for my many outfits which would never fit in the saddle bags. They barely fit in the RV!

The biker culture attracts a diverse group of people from hardcore enthusiasts to weekend warriors, from posers to (you guessed it) Swingers. Our group that year included seven couples, all of whom were Lifestyle friends from our previous travels or friends of friends. The campground we stayed at was 600 acres - the world's largest temporary accommodation location. Thanks to our friends, we managed to get all of the RVs and campers in adjacent campsites with a reserved common area in the middle.

The campground famously featured the infamous Titty Alley — a half a mile road that bisected the campground. It was a hot spot for cruising and we ladies were encouraged to show our "titties" to the admiring throngs of bikers as we cruised the strip. Just like Bourbon Street in New Orleans, girls bared their breasts for colorful beads. And of course, I made sure I brought back a large collection of them.

Nudity was accepted throughout the campground which was both a blessing and a curse: There were hot women everywhere but just as many old bikers enjoying letting it all hang out. And then there were the half-dressed "shirt-cocks" or older men, nude from the waist down with their t-shirts creating an awning for their dangling junk.

We enjoyed the trip so much that we bought our own RV and returned to Sturgis two years later. The second time, our campground featured a pop-up sex shop. I picked up a strap-on that featured a small vibrating dildo for the person wearing it and a larger one for their partner's pleasure. Since the first time I got fucked with a strap-on, it has always turned me on. I was excited to use it as two heads are always better than one... I just didn't imagine who would be on the receiving end.

Buttfuck Nowhere

Josh - On our return trip from Sturgis, we camped at a Walmart Super Center in the middle of rural Idaho. Considering the remote location and the time of night, the parking lot had many cars and there were several other RVs positioned to quietly stay overnight. It was a stark contrast to the loud biker party scene we had just left.

We positioned ourselves away from the store where the parking was easier with a big rig. The sides of the motorhome were popped out to make room in the living area. The shade blinds were down, but the privacy screens were not, so the red LED lighting gave the interior of the RV a sexy, sensual vibe. After a bit of dancing and foreplay, Maggie pulled out one of the new toys and looked at me with a sly, little smile...she was going to make me her bitch.

I've always enjoyed anal play, but the thought of sticking that big dildo up my ass was both exciting and terrifying. The anal workshops we had previously attended, taught us a few things: We knew it was time for a little preparation to relax the sphincter. North, south, east, west, her lubed fingers traced the rim of my ass and occasionally dipped inside me until I was relaxed and ready to receive.

Maggie pulled the strap-on over her hips and gently inserted the smaller dildo into her pussy. The glow of the red light revealed her beautiful feminine curves, her large breasts and... a slightly oversized cock. She looked incredible and powerful.

My virginal ass was about to get stuffed. I got on my knees in front of the sofa and rested my upper body on the cushions, my ass was up and on display, a vulnerable position for someone used to pitching not catching. I knew Maggie's own experiences would have taught her how to receive. She used that knowledge to make me feel safe and she listened to my guidance, "Plenty of lube, go slow and no ground and pound!"

It took a lot of mind control to keep my body relaxed. At first, it was a bit painful but once my inner sphincter muscles relaxed, it was incredible. She had done a good job preparing me.

Our positions were reversed from the usual, with Maggie holding my hips from behind as she slowly pushed and pulled her strap-on in and out of my ass. She thrust into me, rubbing against my prostate with each drive. I stroked my cock to increase my pleasure so it didn't take long for me to have an explosive climax. The pressure on my prostate contributed to a huge load of cum like I had never experienced before.

Being fucked by my wife didn't turn me gay, and it didn't cause me to start thinking about guys. It did allow for a greater understanding of the dynamics of power between the feminine and masculine. I was now the receiver of my lover's penetration both physically and mentally. As the receiver, I had to surrender my body fully in order to truly embrace the pleasure.

For someone so used to giving and inserting sexually, it was a role reversal to be completely vulnerable and allow her to penetrate me. There was the physical act of receiving which was intense and pleasurable but there was also the emotional act of letting go and allowing her to take care of me.

I will never have a pussy and she will never have a cock, but we both have an anus. That hole, with all its nerve endings, is the great equalizer.

Stranger Danger

We really enjoyed the combo of bikes and bangin' at Sturgis so the following year, Josh and I attended the Arizona Bike Week in Scottsdale. Just like with Sturgis, our group had positioned their RVs and trailers to create our private area and chill-out space. One of the couples we met was new to us but knew our other friends well. They wouldn't stay strangers for long.

Josh - One night at the bike rally, an attractive couple caught our eye. They were Veronica and Craig, a cool couple from California and part of the compound that our motorhomes created. Veronica had been the topic of conversation earlier that evening between myself and the guys. She apparently had this special technique that scared most but thrilled a few. It was all relayed through innuendo as we made a point of not kissing and telling. I was intrigued though, and Maggie encouraged me to go talk to Veronica and introduce myself.

Craig and I connected through conversation and I enjoyed his company. After spending some time getting to know each other, they invited us to join them in their 40-foot coach. The conversation got sexier and a short time later, Veronica invited me to the back bedroom leaving Maggie up front with her husband. Veronica immediately took off all my clothes, laid me down, tied me up and blindfolded me. It happened so fast...she was basically a stranger and there I was, completely under her control.

I consumed some cannabis edibles earlier and the THC-fueled excitement was beginning to fill my body, amplifying the moment. As I lay there naked, bound and blindfolded, my imagination and senses were on high alert. I could hear the sounds as she slowly prepared, but I had no idea what was in store for me.

I thought to myself, "Why am I lying in a stranger's RV tied to the bed and naked? Maggie and I like adventure, but is this pushing the limits?" I then heard Veronica approach. She touched my skin and in the darkness, her touch was intensified. She massaged my awaiting skin with cannabis-infused coconut oil and the warmth of her hands spreading the oil helped my body relax.

The massage was wonderful but I sensed she was softening me up for what was to come. She leaned into my ear and whispered something that I couldn't comprehend. Then...I was shocked. Literally shocked. Her touch had turned electric and she masterfully traced my body from head to toe with tingles of energy. My body was a conduit for electrostimulation. It rode the edge of excitement and pain.

I became anxious thinking that she might touch my sensitive balls with a jolt of electricity but she expertly avoided direct contact with my nipples and groin. The sensations were intense and produced thirteen energetic orgasms before I had to tap out.

That night with Veronica was one of the most erotically charged nights I've ever had, and one of the most memorable. Since then we've introduced a number of our friends to the stimulating effects of electricity. It's always a good way to turn up the energy and get a party started.

Friends Helping Friends

Josh and I were feeling an added intensity and passion about the Lifestyle but found it difficult to express it with most of our monogamous friends back home. The sexual freedom that we expressed on our trips didn't translate well with many of them. Some couldn't understand the Lifestyle and expressed it was something they would have a hard time exploring. Remarks such as, "I have a hard enough time with one woman, what would I do with more?" Or, "I could never do that. I'm way too jealous." It was difficult for them to understand what Josh and I were choosing. It felt way too risky for most.

Fortunately, a few of my closest girlfriends had flexible mindsets which allowed me to share all of my wild and crazy encounters. My friend April was one of the open ones. She was an exotic, stunning, blonde with a curvaceous sexy body. (Josh referred to the two of us as MILF's.) Unfortunately, she was in a marriage that lacked the physical touch she craved and saw the opportunity to embrace our Lifestyle. She asked if I could help her get some much needed sexual gratification.

Josh and I pondered her request. The fact that we would be facilitating her "cheating" on her husband wasn't lost on us. It would be against traditional monogamous relationship boundaries. In addition, it diverged from the transparency we had in our relationship and conflicted to the openness we were accustomed to in the Lifestyle. However, it was her responsibility to manage her relationship with her partner, not ours. We justified the idea with the belief that we would be assisting her to fulfill her needs and desires. We agreed to her request.

April loved the idea of me bringing in single guys for afternoon play sessions with just us girls. I would arrange for us to have sex dates with my collection of safe, single men always willing to fulfill our desires. When Josh couldn't be there, he gave us his blessing. At other times, Josh and I would satisfy her itch.

Ultimately, April's marriage failed for a variety of reasons but mostly because he was in love with someone else. We observed that the lack of communication and intimacy in a marriage can lead to its erosion.

One is a Lonely Number

Josh and I had an arrangement when it came to playing separately: If he was working, I could take one of my girlfriends on a play date with another guy. Josh made sure that he had met all the guys previously and was comfortable with them. This made me feel special and loved by Josh.

One sunny afternoon, Diane and I met up with Joey, a super hot young stud. He had invited us for an afternoon of pleasure on his sailboat. We were both excited and ready to get it on with him.

The three of us sat on the upper deck, admiring the beautiful ocean and suntanning in our bikini-clad bodies. After some verbal foreplay, he invited us both below deck. Diane and I stripped off our bikinis and kissed Joey passionately. He was enjoying all the attention but the next thing I knew, Joey took Diane's hand and guided her to his bed.

At that moment, I wasn't sure if I should follow — neither of them looked over or invited me to join. I felt awkward and wasn't sure if I should say anything. Diane straddled Joey — she wanted his cock deep inside her pussy. Neither of them glanced my way. They were so enthralled with each other that it felt too late and too uncomfortable for me to interrupt their flow.

I sat at the dining table and watched them, hoping that, at some point, they would acknowledge me. Feelings of insecurity welled up: Was I not as pretty as her? Was I not as sexy as her? I had cleared my afternoon and thought that I was going to get fucked. I had an expectation and now I felt disappointed and frustrated.

I wasn't going to show them what I was feeling, I just sat back and watched the show. After a quick pounding, they got up from the bed and joined me. They were basking in the afterglow and cuddling. But still, nothing was said to me. I felt invisible. I left that afternoon feeling neglected, although somewhat happy for Diane. I knew she was in a sexless relationship and that she hadn't been fucked for quite some time.

That experience taught me how important it was to be inclusive and aware of all of my play partners. Since that afternoon, I've created more inclusive play times.

I've Been Kidnapped, Don't Help!

Josh - We didn't have to be away from home to experience something unique. For my birthday one year, Maggie was working on a movie and couldn't be present so she arranged to give me a birthday that I wouldn't forget.

I was instructed to be home at noon and leave my afternoon open. I dutifully obliged and at 12 o'clock, the doorbell rang. Our dear friend Stephanie was at the door. She stepped into our foyer and blindfolded me. She whispered into my ear, "You are now under my control." I accepted her demands as my heart beat heavily with anticipation.

She guided me outside the front door and locked it behind us. She led me to her waiting car and directed me into the front seat. I didn't know if we were alone or if there were others in the car. My birthday surprise was getting really exciting.

Silently, she drove me through stop and go traffic. We drove on the freeway, over speed bumps and through residential streets. If anyone looked into the car and saw me blindfolded, I'm sure they'd question my story.

When we finally stopped, she got out and instructed me to stay still until she returned. I obeyed and didn't even peek out from my blinders. A few moments later, she retrieved me from the car and walked me to our journey's end.

Once inside our mystery destination, she turned me around and stripped off all my clothes. She guided me to an object that I immediately recognized as a massage table and commanded me to lie down. I recalled that she had recently purchased a massage table and deduced that we were at her home.

As I lay on the table, she lubed me up with warm oil. Sensual smells filled the air as her loving touch caressed my body. The gentle music relaxed me, still I was aroused. With my vision off-line, my hearing was acute and I heard footsteps approaching on the hardwood. Then I heard another set of footsteps. How many women were headed toward my naked body?

My mind and heart raced: I was in "fight or flight" but I wanted to stay exactly where I was. The footsteps arrived along with the mystery women and I felt the touch of more hands gliding over my well-lubricated body. I surrendered to their touch and welcomed the eroticism, I felt safe and nurtured as eight hands explored my body.

The four women used their bodies and hands to give me an amazing massage and I lost myself in the sensations of their touch. Each one was different and they each fought for my attention. It was an hour of sheer birthday delight.

When they removed my blindfold, I was surrounded by dear friends in another friend's house. We were all aroused so we finished with a mutual masturbation session, all bringing ourselves to climax together. I was so grateful for the day.

Maggie had requested one of the girls send her regular sexts. They took pictures of the event and sent them to her so she could see and be part of the experience. Although she was working, she was turned on by the photos, knowing how much I was enjoying my birthday. Later at home, I got to relive the moment as I shared my memories with her.

When you take jealousy out of the equation, there is infinite creativity to design experiences that are shared by all. Just because Maggie couldn't be there, it didn't mean that I couldn't enjoy myself. I will forever admire my wife's strength and generosity of spirit.

Fantasies...We All Have Them

The Lifestyle provides an opportunity to explore sexual fantasies, so we have allowed ourselves to indulge. It is important for Josh and I to feel secure enough to express our desires to each other. We don't judge the other for our expressions. It can be vulnerable for us to share intimate details of our fantasies, but we make a point of holding space for each other.

Sometimes fantasies are not pre-planned but are a spontaneous response to the situation. The space we allow each other gives us the freedom to take advantage of sexual opportunities as long as they are within the boundaries that we have established. Sometimes our fantasies originate in our own minds and sometimes we are the helping hand (or cock) that fulfills someone else's fantasy.

Josh - Imagine a house party with 20 couples in attendance, each guest dressed to accent his or her best assets: short skirts exposing curvaceous legs, plunging necklines holding in ample breasts, and well-fitted shirts clinging to strong male shoulders. All around the room are flirtatious smiles and sultry eyes.

This was the set-up one New Year's afternoon.

Midway through the day, the hostess, Willow, touched Maggie on her arm and asked if we could help fulfill a fantasy. Maggie's eyebrows raised as she asked, "What kind of fantasy?" Willow's blue eyes glimmered as she answered that she wanted to be a "Hot Wife" for me and Maggie. She didn't need to do anything to be a hot wife, she already was one with her tall, sculpted body and shoulder-length blonde hair. Maggie looked over at me and without hesitation, I nodded in reply.

I looked over at her husband, Blake, and saw the excitement in his eyes. As we joined forces, the arrangements were made - the three of us would be in the master bedroom with her husband just on the other side of the door. The thought of sensual playtime (with Blake within earshot) was tantalizing. As we walked down the hallway I became turned on with anticipation, knowing that I would soon be wrapped in Willow's sexiness.

Once in the bedroom, the clothes were quickly scattered on the floor. She reclined on the king size bed and Maggie moved her face between Willow's heaving breasts, caressing and kissing them until her nipples became erect. I sat back for a moment to savor the vision of two beautiful women engaged in pure pleasure. My hunger for them increased until finally I couldn't resist and I positioned myself next to them.

I began by kissing Willow's silky lips. Then the three of us exchanged deep, passionate kisses. I was so sexually charged that I needed to slow myself down. There was no need to rush, there was plenty to go around. I used my lips to gently kiss Willow's neck then tasted her shoulders with soft licks. My fingertips traced the shape of her breasts as they slowly made their way down to her pussy. She lifted her hips slightly to welcome my touch. My fingers found her wetness as I spread her thighs apart. I wanted to taste and smell her womanhood.

I glanced at Maggie, who looked at me with that knowing smile. I focused all of my energy between Willow's legs. She lifted her thighs over my shoulders and opened herself to my attention. As my tongue traced a figure eight over her clit, I felt it swelling in my wet mouth. I pulled her hard towards me as I flattened my tongue against her. Touching her glistening labia, I teasingly grabbed them in between my fingers and gently massaged them.

I could hear Maggie breathing deeply with excitement as she played with her own breasts. I longed for Maggie as well, and my free hand found her juicy ass, concentrating on the area that I knew made her wetness flow. She felt my attention and responded by moving down the bed, fondling my balls and teasing my cock with her mouth and tongue. Maggie's oral skills always got my attention and I had to balance the sensations of receiving while still paying attention to my other partner. We writhed against each other in pleasure and ecstasy until Willow untangled herself saying, "Be right back." As she disappeared into the bathroom. Maggie and I took the time to reconnect, sharing the flavor of our new friend still wet on my lips.

When Willow rejoined us, she was holding Erosscia, her favorite toy. She handed it to Maggie who placed it against her clit as I slid my cock into her juicy folds. It felt amazing as the vibrations rippled through her swollen labia and brought us waves of intense pleasure. Then Maggie slid the toy's long thin shaft inside, against my throbbing penis. Willow joined *in, playing with Maggie, tugging at her nipples and gliding her hands over Maggie's soft curves. I looked into Maggie's eyes, and we all let out moans of mutual enjoyment. Maggie's whole body began to vibrate, the synergy of the toy, my cock, and Willow's touch, brought her to an intense full-body orgasm. Completely satisfied Maggie collapsed beside me on the bed.*

The sensual energy in the room remained charged and I was still erect as Willow reached over to the nightstand to retrieve a condom. She presented it to me with a coy smile; it was her turn to have me deep inside of her. Always quick to recover, Maggie helped me by sensually and teasingly sliding the rubber over my shaft. I reclined on the mattress as Willow straddled me and slid my cock easily inside her waiting pussy. My wife added to the pleasure by gently fondling my balls and teasing my perineum while I was fucking another beautiful woman. I let out a deep moan as Maggie slipped her finger into my ass and pressed against my prostate.

Willow thrust her hips and pressed her clitoris against my stiff shaft. She rode me hard as she moaned with pleasure. As I watched her breasts swing, our breathing amplified and I knew we were both close to climax. Maggie alternated and kissed us both deeply as we descended into our mutual orgasms.

Content and full of happy hormones, we lay on the bed and like great athletes after an intense workout, we recovered our breath. We gently snuggled until it was time to rejoin the others.

It was fun going back to the party, a little disheveled and with knowing smiles on our faces. I could see the excitement on Blake's face as his hot wife returned to him, smelling of our sex.

To our joy, we received a package in the mail a short time later. Our play friend had sent Maggie her very own Erosscia vibrator, which is now one of her favorite toys.

Happy Endings

Once a year, a temporary city is erected in the middle of the desert in Nevada. Some call it a festival, but Burning Man is more than that. It is based on ten principles, many of which are the antithesis of the values held in our society. These principles are:

F*cking Our Way to Enlightenment

1. Radical Inclusion (all are welcome)
2. Gifting (ask not what I can take from Burning Man, but what I can give)
3. Decommodification (nothing is bought or sold)
4. Radical Self-reliance (bring what you need to survive in the desert - physically, mentally, and emotionally)
5. Radical Self-expression (art, costumes, music, theme camps - the best of the human spirit)
6. Communal Effort (participants are encouraged to volunteer and actively participate)
7. Civic Responsibility (the opposite of individualism, valuing the welfare of all participants)
8. Leave No Trace (stewardship for the environment and leaving the location trash free and in a better state than found)
9. Participation (BM is not for wallflowers)
10. Immediacy (bringing one's multi-dimensional self and deeply experiencing the event)

Burning Man had been on Josh's bucket list for many years and we had Lifestyle friends from around the USA and Canada who were equally intrigued. We decided to form a group and meet at the event. We created a theme camp called "Kinkster Camp" with all of our RVs and trailers forming a circle around our shade and party structure.

Our friend, Jenny, had been to Burning Man the previous year and told me about a theme camp that gave erotic sensual massages. Jenny had received a happy ending massage from Sean and his work came highly recommended. That sounded right up my alley so the two of us got on our bikes and rode across the playa to where the camp was located. As luck would have it, Sean was there again and greeted me openly, wearing just a pair of drawstring pants and army boots.

I was handed a contract to sign. It was a document that listed all the ways Sean might be touching me. As I read through the consent form, it became clear that I was comfortable with him touching my breasts, ass and vagina. The act of ticking off the boxes was making me wet so I knew there was no argument from my pussy.

Sean escorted me behind the curtain, then asked me to remove all of my clothing and lie face up on the massage table. He gave me a set of headphones and put a set on himself, explaining that we'd both be listening to the same music. The massage would be 50-minutes long. Blindfolded.

I was equally excited and nervous but with the slow, soothing symphony, I began to relax. I couldn't hear anything except for the headphones so when Sean's warm, soft hands touched my stomach, it startled me. He slowly made his way to my breasts, caressing and massaging them gently.

Being blindfolded made the physical sensations more pronounced so when Sean's hands paused on my pussy, a tingling, warm sensation came over me. He moved on to my legs and then to my ankles. As he held my foot and massaged each of my toes, my breath quickened and I became more aroused.

The music shifted from classical to modern as it resonated through my head and my body. He remained the conductor and played my body as if it were an instrument. At times, he would tap lightly to the sound of drums beating, then switch to scratching my body lightly, then back to tapping. As he moved his percussive fingertips toward my mound, my pussy was silently squealing for attention. I felt more and more energy rush through my body and into my labia.

The music changed again and I felt a light spritz of cool mist being sprayed all over my body. It was an immersive, 4-D massage. As the sounds of the cymbals reached a crescendo, my arousal increased and I shivered with ecstasy. I couldn't hold my body still and I undulated my back and hips to the music.

I wondered, "How much more can I endure?" As if by response, I felt warm oil pour all over my body. Sean's hands and arms lightly pressed on top of my stomach and worked their way down to my vulva. More warm oil was poured on my pussy lips. Finally, she was getting the attention she craved. I twinged and let out a gasp.

Sean placed his fingers between my folds as he gently massaged and flicked my clit. Another gasp and I moaned quietly. He penetrated my pussy with his warm fingers, moving them slowly inside, increasing his speed to match the faster and louder music. My groans became loud and I knew I was close to cumming. "Oh God, Oh God," I shouted. When his lips sucked, kissed and gently bit my nipples it sent me over the edge. I let out a scream of pleasure and sexual release.

As the grand finale, Sean used his pussy-drenched fingers to open my lips and spray whipped cream into my awaiting mouth. I laughed at the unexpected surprise and licked the sweet cream and my own cream off my lips. He took off my blindfold, and asked, "How was that?"

Please, Sir, could I have some more?

I wanted more pleasure, so I asked, "Can you make me squirt?" Sean smiled at me and answered, "Yes."

I positioned myself on my knees on the massage table. With his body close to mine, I could feel his excitement rising as well. He put his two fingers inside my hungry pussy and massaged the inner walls of my vagina. I called out, " Faster, faster...Harder, harder." Within seconds, his expert touch made me squirt down my inner thighs, and onto the vinyl table as I screamed with release and total satisfaction.

I opened my eyes and looked at Sean, saying, "Thank you for the amazing erotic, sensual experience. It was the best I've ever had." He responded "My pleasure" and I could tell that it was.

It took me a few minutes to clean up and get dressed. My whole body was energized and tingling. My legs felt like rubber and I could barely walk but when I emerged from behind the curtain, my girlfriend said, "The whole camp heard you. Women stopped to listen to your sounds of pleasure and many booked a massage. Immediately." Nothing like an acoustic business card.

I was excited to share my experience with Josh and to gift him (and others) the pleasure of a 4-D sensory massage. That one experience at Burning Man had encapsulated most of the Burning Man principles, but I definitely left a trace. Or two.

Full Service Limo

Our friend, Nick, was a limo driver and one day he suggested that I get a couple of friends together and have some fun in his stretch limo. Nick was a 6' 5" muscle-bound, black, sexy man so there was nothing about this plan that I didn't like.

Neither Josh nor I had ever played in a limo before, so we were both excited at the prospect. We were always open to finding new places to fuck in groups. I asked my girlfriend Patsy if she wanted to join in the fun and bring her boyfriend Ross. I liked him, he had a great cock and he was sexy and talented in bed. Not surprisingly, they both answered with a resounding, "Yes!"

Josh was working late that day, so Nick picked up Patsy, Ross, and myself at my house, leaving Josh to catch up with us later. With excitement, we loaded the limo with all the things that we'd need for the night of fun. It was a limo, so we included champagne.

Nick drove us to a large city park and found a secluded area to pull over. Once parked, he climbed into the back to join us. We cranked up the music and opened the bubbles. Our clothes came off and we quickly got hot and charged up. As we waited for Josh's arrival, Patsy and I reclined on the seats, opened our legs and invited Nick and Ross to pleasure our pussies. Soon all the windows in the limo had steamed up and we heard a knock.

Josh - There was a hiccup in our limo plans when I had to work later than normal. I suggested to Maggie that they didn't need to wait and should start without me. The last hours at work were exciting for me as I thought of her in the back of the limo being pleasured by our friends. It heightened the anticipation rather than dampening it.

When I was finally ready to leave, I sent Maggie a text to find out where they were. It didn't take long to locate them, the stretch limo stuck out from the few other cars parked on the secluded road.

From the outside of the vehicle, the steamy inside wasn't apparent because of the tinted windows. When I opened the door, I saw the four of them naked and fully engaged. It's a good thing that I wasn't a cop.

Their earlier sexts had me ready to go so I jumped right in. The five of us fucked and sucked while unknowing cars passing by within feet of our limo orgy. At one point, I looked up to see a wide-eyed Nick...Ross was giving Nick a blowjob and he wasn't sure about receiving it. Fortunately, Nick accepted the attention of another man without taking offence. It could have escalated quickly, but never amounted to more than a star-

tled expression. Personally, I enjoyed watching the action and admired that they were both secure in their sexuality enough to share the erotic expression.

Let's face it - if Ross was headed towards Nick's cock and he didn't want that type of male attention, he could have graciously declined with a simple, "Thank you, but no thank you" and the flow would have continued in another direction. Period. It's best to know your limits and play within them, as the lotto ad says.

Guy-on-guy play isn't very typical in the Lifestyle and it doesn't always cross the mind of the participants. Desires for that type of play should be expressed prior to play. Good communication is key to enjoyable playtimes.

It Takes a Village to Raise a...Couple

Our twentieth anniversary landed on Canada Day so Josh booked a beautiful suite overlooking the ocean with an amazing view of the upcoming fireworks. We planned some fireworks of our own and invited a few of our Lifestyle friends to join us for an evening of sex and appies.

There were four couples and two single girlfriends, all gathered to celebrate our marriage and the life that we created together. We opened a couple of bottles of champagne and toasted each other, happy with our choice of life partner. We both felt blessed that we embraced the road less traveled.

With cultural norms, an anniversary celebration is reserved for the two people involved (but as always) we saw no need to limit our enjoyment to the two of us. We began the evening by kissing and caressing each other while letting the rest flow naturally. Some guests wanted to watch, while others quickly got naked on the bed. We were surrounded by our tribe, and close to those who understood our take on life, pleasure, sex, and relationships. Josh and I shared our love and commitment towards our marriage, knowing that casual sex does not waver us in any way.

Fresh Meat Monday

Josh and I loved the theme nights that many hosts select for their Lifestyle parties. They challenged us to use our creativity and design sexy, coordinated costumes for the evening's festivities. Some of the themes we've dressed for were: Fetish Night, Sexy Red Night, Glam Party, Sultry 70s, ABC Party, Back to School, Leather & Lace and Neon. The existence of a theme changed the whole tone of the night and we loved the possibility of role-playing.

I enjoyed fashion and was skilled at sewing so I created costumes for myself and Josh. I always tied the look together with makeup and wigs. I loved that I could attend parties incognito. The evening became a performance and I would transform into any persona that I desired. Sometimes even our closest friends couldn't recognize me in costume.

On one particular trip to Hedo, my quick change skills shocked and surprised a couple of our new playmates. One afternoon mid-way through our stay, I met New Yorker Nicole by the pool who told me about her firefighter husband. She was a hot nurse, 10 years younger than us and full of energy. She confessed to having a sensational sex drive which led to a quickie make out session by the pool.

As the sunlight waned, Josh and I went back to our room to change into our theme party clothes. I covered my own short hair with a platinum, braided wig that cascaded over my breasts. I slid into my come-fuck-me high heels and slipped into my tight, lace mini dress. I looked hot and ready to be fucked.

We went to dinner with a few other couples that we had met earlier that day. After dinner, I excused myself to go to the bathroom. As I stood in the mirror applying my red lipstick, I noticed New Yorker Nicole who was touching up her makeup next to me. She looked over at me and said, "OMG, you are so hot." She had no idea that we had made out only hours before. She then asked if we would like to get together with her and her husband. Knowing that she was *definitely* Josh's type, I answered yes.

I quickly walked back to the dining room table and told Josh about my bathroom encounter and that we were invited to Nicole and

Matt's hotel suite. Josh was excited, remembering the afternoon by the pool. Because of my transformation, she didn't recognize me, but I knew that the reveal would be fun.

We arrived at their room and off came our clothes. Matt was well built, super toned and really sexy. Nicole was a tall, blonde with a tight body that Josh was equally eager to explore. The sexual charge was palpable.

The sex part happened quickly...Josh was on the bed and Nicole was on top, riding his cock fast and hard. I was on the other side of the bed with Matt on top, thrusting his big cock inside of me. Despite all the sexual activity going on, we still maintained conversations. Nicole said, "I haven't seen you two around the hotel." I reintroduced myself and reminded her that she and I had been making out by the pool. She burst out laughing and then started lightly punching Josh on the chest as if to inform him of her realization. Then she said, "I can't believe it - I thought you guys were fresh meat!" Apparently, Josh's sunglasses and hat that afternoon had hidden his identity well enough that they didn't tie us together.

She persisted and wouldn't stop talking and laughing about it until finally, Matt turned to her in his Brooklyn accent, saying, "Would you just shut-the-fuck-up already? I'm trying to fuck right now." We laughed but it took us a few minutes to get back in the groove again. I was the ultimate quick change artist.

The Pleasures of Pussy

As the years went on, I was noticing that most men in their late 40s and 50s were not vital super studs any more. When Josh and I would find a hot-looking couple and take them back to a hotel suite for some playtime, so many of the men just couldn't get hard. I wasn't getting the response that I was used to but I sensed that it wasn't me. Their excuses ranged from being too tired, too nervous, or too intoxicated. Despite all the excuses, the fact remained that my playtime was left unfinished, although Josh continued to enjoy himself with the women.

I didn't resent my husband's continued enjoyment, but I needed to do something to ensure my own satisfaction so I switched gears and spent more time with the women. This wasn't just for sexual gratification, I was also beginning to feel a deeper connection to other females. Women were opening up to me as I was to them. The touch of another woman was turning me on more and more. Sometimes it was tricky for me to relate to females since I had a husband and only sons. I didn't have a close relationship with my mother nor did I have any sisters, so this left my life lacking in female energy.

It was becoming the norm to bring toys and vibrators to our play sessions. I recall the first time that a female lover introduced to a double-ended penis vibrator. It was incredibly erotic and made me climax so easily. Feeling the soft sensuous body of another woman and kissing her beautiful breasts and lips was such a turn-on for me. I never realized how much I was missing out on spending time with another female.

Eventually, Josh and I found ourselves drawn to single women. Our playtimes would be more than just a quickie, many lasting several hours. We realized that we were both more satisfied with our female-centered play sessions. Josh enjoyed watching the heightened sexual energy between me and other women. My turn-on was amplified when I saw Josh get hard as he watched me play.

Josh was such a gentleman, never forcing himself on the other women. He just waited until we were either finished or invited him in to play. I could sense the women were comfortable and felt safe around him. This allowed the three of us to flow our energies with ease and without expectations.

We had no idea what other changes were in store for us on our sexual journey together.

No More Groundin' and Poundin'

Maybe it's because Josh and I were getting older or maybe it was that the novelty was wearing off, but the ground and pound started to become a bit "boring." It lacked the attraction or the rewards that it used to have when we first joined the Lifestyle. There were only so many new and exciting places and ways that we could have sex in groups and once we tried many, many of them, the excitement wanes.

We began looking for a greater connection with our play friends. Our style had changed and become slower, more connected and less, "Wham, bam, thank you, Ma'am." It became important for us to take the time and explore every inch of our play partners' bodies, from the top of their head to the tip of their toes. We enjoyed using a light touch with our fingertips and nails, or sometimes we liked to lick, kiss or just breathe all over their bodies. We would map out their body in our minds, noting which areas, other than the genitals, were erogenous. The more time that was built up in anticipation, the more it drew awareness across the entire body. That way the other person would more likely experience full-body pleasure.

Most partners would naturally hold their breath when they were about to climax, but we would encourage our play partners to fully inhale and exhale to ramp up their pleasure. When we used long, deep breaths, it allowed us to stay in the moment, deepening our sensations. It was important for us to make noises too. We would scream out, groan, moan, grunt, or just whisper into each other's ears. The more we expressed through vibrational sound, the better. The higher-pitched sounds would activate the energy located on the top of the head, forehead and throat. The lower sounds would resonate in the heart, upper abdomen, lower belly and perineum. Some women liked to slowly squeeze and release the Kegel muscles (the ones that stop the flow of urine). I liked to spread my legs open and undulate my lower back to increase the flow of energy moving it up my spine.

With our newfound skills and approaches to playtime, I saw a definite change in how we interacted with our play partners. It was a new adventure and for us, anything new was going to be exciting and pleasurable. We would make it so. After all, we were Pleasure Seeking Adults.

Knowing others
is wisdom.
Knowing yourself
is enlightenment.

- Lao Tzu

F*cking Our Way to Enlightenment

From Sport Fucking to Sacred Energy Sharing

Josh and I were slowly emerging from our Covid-19 cocoon and we were delighted to entertain Lana, a beautiful single woman and a casual friend of twenty years. The late afternoon sun was warm as we sat around our outdoor living space. I treated us with some of my homemade kombucha and appies and she treated us to her stories from the previous two years. It was refreshing to have a guest in our home once again.

We were excited to show Lana our new meditation and playroom space that we had created during the lock down. The main attraction was a large pillow-covered bed in one corner of the room. We covered the walls with mandala tapestries and fabrics, with light blue sheers draped from the ceiling and lighting that gave the impression of being underwater. Flowing red velvet curtains covered the windows and a soft white, fluffy rug lay on the floor completing the sensual bohemian decor.

Lana immediately flopped herself down on the bed and took in the ambiance. We were all enjoying the vibe and decided to settle into the room for the evening. I added to the mood by lighting a few candles and lit a stick of my favorite Nag Champa incense on the side table. Josh put on one of his favorite playlists and adjusted the lighting.

We talked with Lana about our recent exploration of sexual energy. She was intrigued and wanted to know more. We took a few minutes for our consent talk so she could express her fears and concerns. She expressed her thoughts then allowed us to share our new techniques. We sat on the bed facing each other, holding hands and eye gazing. We became present and established a 3-way connection. As we practiced mindful breathing, the connection deepened.

The room was heating up and so were we. Our clothes became a barrier, so we disrobed to our undergarments. We lay back, with Lana in the middle, a delectable filling to our sandwich. She was slender with perky breasts, her active lifestyle evident in her shapely muscles. I asked her if I could touch her body, and she responded with an affirming, "Yes." I gently stroked her skin, taking my time to slowly trace every curve of her sexy body. I could feel her responding to my touch, as she rose slightly to meet my fingertips.

Josh met my eyes as I gently caressed Lana's breasts. He was enjoying watching me explore what gave her pleasure. I lightly kissed Lana on her lips and she responded by reciprocating, kissing me deeply. I nuzzled into her neck and whispered into her ear, "You are so beautiful and sexy."

Josh moved in closer and asked Lana for consent to touch her. She nodded and gave him a little smile. He stroked her hair and caressed her face and upper chest, always listening for her verbal responses and watching how her body responded to his touch. Slowly his hands traveled down her body as he moved to the end of the bed. He sat on his knees and reached over to the nightstand to get some coconut oil. He scooped some out and melted it between his hands before he caringly massaged Lana's feet and legs. Then his oily hands made their way over to me; using one hand on each of us, he worked his way up our legs as we moaned with pleasure. The addition of Lana was creating a trilogy of turn-on.

Josh's hands continued up our legs until he reached our panties. He cupped his hands on top of our silk-covered pelvic mounds and held still, unmoving. I felt my clit swelling to the warmth of his touch, and based on Lana's sounds, she must have been feeling the same. Her breathing increased in tempo as she slightly raised her hips. Whatever sex magic was emitting from his hands increased our arousal even further. He followed the energy up our bodies with his hands, pausing momentarily to concentrate on each of our chakra points. When he reached the top of our crowns, I sat up and kissed him passionately, sending tingles and shivers up both of our bodies. To tune into each other, Josh and I matched our breathing. I put my right hand on Josh's heart and my left hand on Lana's heart. As we breathed together, we melded into a deep connection. Josh's body was responding with quick jolts of energy. We kissed and our tongues danced together, I could feel the Kundalini energy rising from the depths of my groin, moving up my central spinal channel and to the crown of my head. My breathing slowed and my body swayed with the force of my sexual energy.

I relaxed my stomach and took deep breaths into my lower dantian as I recognized an orgasm building. I felt multiple waves of life force energy rise within me. I was moving towards having a mind orgasm and kept my intention on my circular breathing, in and out with no pause between. The more I maintained that breathing pattern, the more pleasure I felt. When I released sounds of pleasure, my state of bliss increased. I couldn't hold it any longer, the orgasm wanted to explode. The energy pulsing through me felt the same as the climax I get when Josh is physically inside of me.

I could see Josh was feeling my climax and began releasing his own mindgasm. He was twitching and shaking with pleasure, reaching a full-on orgasm but without ejaculation.

I leaned over to kiss Lana, who had been watching us intently, observing our sex. She closed her eyes and slowly moved her hand down her belly, sliding it under the waistband of her silk panties. She gently teased her fingers over her mound and circled over her hard clit. I snuggled into her soft neck, watching the strain of the fabric over her hand as she skillfully gave herself pleasure.

Her pace increased as did her breathing. Lana couldn't hold back any longer as she surrendered herself to her two fingers, fervently rubbing her needy clit. Faster and faster she moved over herself, stopping only to dip her fingers into her wet pussy to add her private lube. We could see she was in her own world as she brought herself to orgasm; a surge of energy jolted through her body as she let out sounds of pleasure.

Witnessing each other's sexual expression felt deeply intimate. With Lana in the middle again, we were delighted to bask in the afterglow of our erotic experience. The silence was broken when Lana giggled and said, "That was the best sex I've ever had without penetration." Josh and I were really enjoying this new play style and knew we had to share it with more friends.

But Once Again, That's Getting Ahead of Ourselves

Throughout our Lifestyle years, we were never drawn towards the party drugs circling the Lifestyle community. A good tequila was Josh's choice as a social lubricant, while I mostly enjoyed a nice glass of red wine. But the occasional afternoon drinking would lead to a siesta before the 5 pm ground and pound parties, and we slowly moved away from it. Cannabis was our favorite mood-altering substance when we were at home. Once it became legal, Josh started growing our own supply. Talking to his plants and giving blessings every day was part of his ritual. When we gave up alcohol, we used cannabis more frequently.

Through our social circles, Josh heard about another plant medicine called DMT (Dimethyltriptamine - aka The God molecule). It's a naturally occurring chemical compound found in many plants and animals, including humans. DMT has been used in religious ceremonies in some South American regions for centuries and because we were deepening our connection to the Divine, we were both curious. The social media algorithms were working overtime and there were many DMT and plant medicine videos for viewing. They got his interest.

Our curiosity collided with opportunity when friends of ours (who are skilled facilitators) offered to hold space for us while we journeyed with DMT. We set ourselves up in our living room and took time to meditate and acknowledge our intentions for the experience. We had borrowed a special pipe and we each took our turn while the others remained close and observed. Soon it was my turn. One hit later and I was launched into another existence. I had never experienced anything like this. It was a world full of sacred geometric patterns, shapes, other-worldly bodies and vibrant colors. Then I became immersed in what I can only describe as a "love soup." I recall telling Josh not to worry, that the tears streaming down my face were of joy and happiness. I had felt pure love and never felt so immersed in it. My heart was full.

Although the trip was less than 10 minutes by the clock, in relative time, it felt like hours. I was blasted to a plane beyond time. It was life-changing. It was profound. It was indescribable. Immediately, *everything* changed.

DMT was where my journey of self-discovery truly began. Luckily, Josh had a similar earth-shattering experience. We wanted to know more.

For years, Josh and I had talked about sitting in an ayahuasca ceremony but until we did DMT (the active chemical in aya), it remained a casual curiosity. After our experience, we felt strongly drawn to ayahuasca - the sacred brew known for expanding one's consciousness. We booked a week at *Rythmia* in Costa Rica, a luxury, medically licensed spiritual retreat. That week, we participated in four plant medicine ceremonies, breath work, yoga and integration sessions. We left with a new perspective on our lives and relationships.

Plant medicines, when honored and used with intention, can reveal the hidden shadow self, as well as teach lessons that would have taken years of therapy to understand. Although neither of us revealed any deep darkness at that time, we did experience some profound realizations... It helped us to understand whom we had become and where our choices had led us.

When we returned from our trip to Costa Rica, we began to question our participation in the Lifestyle. It wasn't that we were turned off of sex, but our priorities had shifted. The plant medicines we ingested induced an ego dissolution or ego death. Ego dissolution allowed us to realize that our identities were built largely upon experiences and things but none of these represented who we truly were. The "ego" or sense of ourselves was a creation of our minds, a mere fabrication.

We began questioning everything that could be ego-driven, including our decision to be Swingers.

We were at the beginning of a spiritual reawakening. Josh and I realized more about our true nature, and as the importance of our ego shifted, we abided in a place of more light and love. We felt better in this higher vibrational state. Soon we were asking, "Why were we seeking sex from others? Were we not satisfied with each other?"

I didn't need or want distractions while I integrated back into society, and the Lifestyle felt like a distraction at that point. Josh felt the same way so we started reading more esoteric books. Our friend circles changed and topics like non-duality, spirituality and the matrix were discussed at length. Our "woo-woo" scale was trending upwards and we were once again on another life path. My priority was to discover who my true authentic self was, beyond being a daughter, a wife, a mother, and a lover.

During the integration phase, Josh and I changed in so many ways:
- We became more intimate in what we shared with each other.
- We encouraged more self-love in our lovemaking sessions
- We became more balanced and grounded, and we were discovering our Divine masculine and feminine energies.
- We felt the need to stop drinking alcohol and we changed our eating habits to a vegetarian diet. We wanted to have a clear mind and healthy body and decided it was a good direction to go.
- We began to see ourselves as a magnet that naturally attracted like-minded people without the need for pretense. Instead of just trying to make ourselves physically attractive, we would be ourselves in social gatherings and allow our inner self to shine. We became more genuine in our interactions with others. Josh and I didn't need to try so hard to meet new open-minded people — we were emitting a frequency of energy that would resonate with certain others who would then find us attractive at an emotional and spiritual level. This universal law was not new but because we had changed, we attracted different types of people.

Our week-long ayahuasca retreat in Costa Rica also changed my mindset about my body. Because my focus shifted from body-centered to energy-centered, it changed my relationship to everything. I no longer stepped on the scale daily. I felt so free. When I felt my weight changing, I would adjust the food I was eating and step up my workout routine. I didn't let my weight control my life.

But, I still had remnants of body issues. I have never allowed Josh to take nude photographs of me. I could look at the animated me in a mirror but I hated looking at myself naked in a photo. All I could see were my imperfections. When the camera came out, I made sure that I grabbed some lingerie.

One evening in our Cauldron of Consciousness (aka hot tub), I felt it was time to finally love myself from the inside out so I asked Josh to videotape me naked. I wanted to look at that video with love in my eyes, not judgment.

I got out of the hot tub and lay on the outdoor couch. Feeling my nervousness, I consciously breathed through it. Once relaxed, I spread my legs, licked my fingers, and played with myself. I felt the anxiety return...If my twenty-year-old self had seen my sixty-year-old self at that moment, she would have been mortified, but I was ready to let go of all those years of self-criticism.

I stared into Josh's eyes. I knew his smile was one of pure pleasure and I could feel his love and affection for me. I kept my thoughts aligned with his thoughts. I got aroused and slowly my fears and hang-ups dissolved. I played with myself until I felt the explosion of a full orgasm. I noticed Josh had a huge grin on his face and a hard cock. He said, "That was one of the sexiest moments I've ever seen, and we've shared many. It will be in my spank bank forever."

When I watched the playback, I saw how beautiful, erotic, and sensual I was. My slight regret is that it took me so many years to realize.

Mid-life Changes - Body and Mind

As I entered menopause, my spiritual changes dovetailed with my physical and emotional changes. I felt more capable, grounded, and sure of myself despite the emotional roller coaster. I let go of that little girl who needed the approval of the group, the one who grew into the woman who wanted to be desired by many. I was learning that the only approval I needed was that of myself.

My body shape was changing and I was going to embrace it. For many women, the switch from being the young, sexy female (of child-bearing years) is super challenging. I felt comfort knowing I had support from my girlfriends in the Lifestyle who were going through the change as well. Some were finding their own way by going under the knife to change and modify their bodies. I just kept up my exercise routines, ate healthily and embraced my body as best as possible. It was an attitude change for sure.

I began daily meditation, journaling, stretching, and Qi Gong. I enjoyed walking and forest bathing. I felt more loving and open to myself and others. My intuition became clearer. Despite all of my self-care practices, I felt that I still wasn't fully connected to my body.

Various spiritual healers had told me that my lower chakras were blocked. It was time for this to change, so I contacted my dear friend Luna Ceovelli, a gifted healer. She specializes in family constellation work and she helped me unpack some of the trauma in my family lineage.

During the session, I felt the fears and the sexual blocks from my grandmother that were locked in my body. Luna explained that physical traits aren't the only ones that are passed down through families; energetic traits and traumas are also inherited as proven through many experiments with epigenetics. It was time for me to release the denser energies that I had inherited.

Luna thought it may take a few more healing sessions to completely remove the block, but I was certain it had been released from my body. And I was right...while practicing my daily meditation in bed the next morning, my body started to shiver. Then I began shaking. I could feel energy building up in my lower abdomen. I followed the energy and swayed my spine. Pleasure overtook me as I moaned and groaned with delight. I took deeper and deeper breaths, feeling the sensation rising up my spine to the crown of my head. I was having a full-body orgasm.

I rode the orgasmic wave for minutes. My face, hands and feet were tingling and a wave of rapture rolled over my back and thighs. I was experiencing my first no-touch, full-body orgasm. Who knows how long it lasted, but I felt rejuvenated and energized when it ended.

I was excited to share what I had experienced. I ran downstairs and cried with excitement. As Josh and I embraced I relayed my incredible orgasmic moment. For most of my life, I experienced pleasure in relation to other people and I shared sexual pleasure with partners. This time was different, there was no physical touch. This marked the first time that I felt pleasure so completely by myself, for myself. Josh had experienced that type of orgasm a few years earlier. He would try to explain his Tantra practice to me and how to let the energy roll throughout my whole body. I didn't understand what that meant. That day, I understood.

Discovering New Energy

Throughout my adult life, I considered sex purely in its physical form. I believed it was meant for pleasure and procreation. I soon discovered that it was a powerful energy with enormous potential that went far beyond the physical limitations of our bodies. After Josh and I journeyed with plant medicines, we began to experience sex as pure cosmic energy and we saw it as a way to connect us to the Divine. Sex allowed us to transcend ourselves in ways that no other experience could. We continued to explore "sex as a sacred practice." We were done with the "ground and pound."

When Covid-19 hit our part of the world in the spring of 2020, it forced us into isolation. Since the Swinger Lifestyle and isolation are mutually exclusive, it compelled us to rethink why we were choosing what we were choosing. We spent more time talking, researching, and learning. We explored the incredible energies that surrounded us. We questioned how to be more present. We realized sex was something sacred and it opened up a new intimacy in our relationship we never knew existed. Although difficult for many, quarantine gifted us a deeper connection that we may have not experienced had our lives not been disrupted.

During the lock down, we both retired from our previous careers and started a new business, using what was imposed on us as a pivot point. We continued to make time to deep dive into our sexuality and spirituality. For six weeks we took at least 90 minutes every other day for sexploration with each other. It was an experiment to discover and try to create a deeper energetic connection. We were mostly making it up as we went along which seemed to be our regular MO. Josh had discovered his abilities to harness these energies earlier and I wanted to understand and control them as well.

A few years into the Lifestyle, one of our male play friends had intrigued Josh with his ability to have orgasms that didn't require penetration, masturbation or ejaculation. The friend's ability fascinated Josh and he wanted to know more about it. Josh's body didn't come with an instruction manual that he could refer to, so he learned through observation, experience and making it up along the way. It didn't take long for him to harness his orgasmic energy so he could be a great partner to me and our playmates, but it has taken years for him to finally understand and control it.

My experience was different. I couldn't get "out of my head" and wouldn't allow orgasms to happen organically. I always needed clitoral stimulation to get me off.

Our previous sexual experiences were more carnal. Our new direction was a deeper, energetic connection (not something that normally exists in an orgy). We needed to concentrate on ourselves and our connection without distraction.

A New Path of Discovery

Josh and I were first exposed to Tantric sexuality during our early years together. We had been married for only a few years and were already looking for ways to spice up our lovemaking skills. We picked up a book on Tantric sex and dove into the practice.

We found it underwhelming and we wondered what all the fuss was about. Our young minds didn't understand the concepts, and it seemed in opposition to the Christian framework to which we were accustomed. How could this painfully slow process of fucking be any more satisfying than a good hard pounding? We were still in the "Wham Bam" phase so we put the book away. We weren't ready. Yet.

Maybe our subconscious minds never forgot those techniques because decades later, Josh and I fell back into the practices.

We are not here to teach about Tantra. We are not teachers of the age-old practices or the Neo-Tantric adaptation of the practices. (Our favorite books on Tantra and Sacred Sexuality are included in the resources section.) This book is about our open relationship and being open to other people is just one of the ways in which we are open. We are also open to practices that add to our connection and to our experience of being human. Tantra has been one of these practices. By slowing down our sexual connection and adding breathwork, we have been able to access levels of our connection that we would not have experienced otherwise. We are multi-dimensional beings and sport fucking represented only one of the aspects of our being.

We haven't devoted decades to studying the practice, but the time that we have devoted has created more pleasure, a deeper connection, expansion, and happiness in our lives. For us, Neo-Tantra is about sexploration, enjoyment and empowerment. It's the opposite of a quickie, and after years of exploring the Lifestyle and its pleasurable yet notably fast-food sex, Josh and I were both wanting to savor our love-making. It was the next step in our sexual journey together.

Neo-Tantra takes the experience of uniting two (or more) people's energies beyond the physical. It involves being present and enjoying the intimacy between one's self and the other(s). Neo-Tantra takes the destination (the orgasm) out of the equation and focuses on the sexual journey, the sensations, and the build-up of passion in the whole body. Using breathwork and intention, the sexual energy flows throughout the body for connection, healing, transformation, and self-awareness. In essence, Neo-Tantra allows for access to wider consciousness by meeting in the still space of presence, the space between thoughts, the space beyond the physical body.

Josh and I have always been sensitive to the energies of others, especially while sharing intimacy, and Tantra was the perfect application to explore them. But we didn't have to give up the destination/the orgasm. The good news is that by making the journey the primary focus, the result was more powerful, full-body orgasms. That's right - the toe-curling, arched back, and O-face type orgasms. The more time and effort that we put into our Neo-Tantric practice, the higher and more intense form of ecstasy we obtained.

Part of our practice includes erotic, erogenous massage. For me, this could include massaging and stroking of my G-spot and cervix together with squeezing and stroking of my inner and outer labia and perineum. It helps me to link my mind with my body. This releases an uncontrollable flow of sexual energy which may be conserved to enhance vitality and Qi (life force energy). In other words, with the right technique, it can be accessed as an energy source more powerful than a Starbucks coffee.

Josh - My full-body orgasms resemble a medical emergency so to avoid concern, I have begun to prepare new playmates by informing them that I am not having a seizure but something much more enjoyable. "Whatever you do, don't call 911."

These intense energy orgasms can be experienced without an erection. How? Energy follows my thoughts, so I practice moving and feeling energy by focusing attention on different parts of my body. Circulating breath and energy with my partner cultivates a deep connection between us. When I am truly in sync with a partner, I am totally physically and energetically connected to our touch. I can direct the flow of primal sexual energy into my heart and throughout my body.

I visualize the physical connection as I glide my fingertips over my partner's skin. I imagine tiny little electrical sparks arching from my fingertips like little Tesla coils. When I am receiving head, I see the lips around my penis and notice every sensation that they bring. I follow my lover's touch with my attention. I see my shaft sliding in and out of her pussy, ass or mouth. No matter what the activity is, I am totally absorbed and present. Every little action heightens my experience.

Light physical stimulation, like scratching the skin, can help me be more present. By focusing on particular areas of the body, I intentionally move the energy around to other places in my body. Everything starts with energy. I have a couple of places where the energy starts to manifest — the first is on my right leg, close to my knee. Why there? I have no idea. I usually control the sensation and move it around my body.

The feelings of euphoria, and the involuntary muscle contractions all occur the same way as during a conventional orgasm. The benefit is that there is no refractory period or recharge time which allows me to experience multiple orgasms in a row. The sensations that are experienced can vary greatly, from mini-gasms to full-body super-O's that roll from one part of my body to another and can last for several minutes. My good orgasms are really an energy (Qi) phenomenon more than a physical one. But when I am able to combine a physical orgasm and an energetic one, I have hit the jackpot.

In the afterglow, I typically experience several little orgasmic jolts that slowly diminish in intensity. This is when I enjoy the sexual bliss and contentment in the warm embrace of my partner.

If We Build It, They Will Cum

As the Covid-19 pandemic proceeded to make our world smaller, the weather changed and autumn rolled in. Our daily hot tub talk sessions were interrupted by the rainy season and we found ourselves communicating less. Determined to find a solution to the problem, we brainstormed and came up with the idea of the Zen Den — a unique room in our home that we could use for meditation, play and self-care.

We wanted our den to be separate from the personal space that was our bedroom. We wanted our den to have its own vibe and spirit. We wanted our den to be a meeting space for our bodies and souls. With all of these goals in mind, we renovated an unused room and created the "set and setting" for our newfound sexplorations.

We are often surprised at the psychological and physiological responses that we and others experienced in our Zen Den. The decor, music, soft lighting, and smell of incense all combined to create a sexy, sensual environment. The feelings of comfort and safety are essential when playing with others, especially when they are both physically and emotionally naked.

Awakening My Kundalini

During my ayahuasca journey, I experienced a form of energetic awakening that led to transformation on the mental, emotional, and spiritual levels. I didn't know it then but what I experienced was a Kundalini awakening.

Kundalini is a Sanskrit word that means "she who is coiled" and refers to the life force energy contained at the base of the spine. It is often represented in the form of a snake. Once this serpentine energy is "awoken," it travels up the various energy centers (or chakras) of the body and into the crown chakra (top of the head) allowing for an expansion in consciousness. The result of this higher awareness is a greater understanding of one's soul, life purpose, and the nature of reality itself. That is why my ayahuasca experience changed everything.

Every Tuesday and Thursday, Josh and I attend Kundalini yoga at a Sikh temple. This practice keeps our bodies tuned into the life force energies while bringing a new dimension into our intimate relations. Although the Kundalini is considered a divine feminine energy, it shouldn't be considered something that only females experience.

I have found Yoga, Reiki, and Qi Gong have been beneficial in strengthening my connection to the parts of myself that are not purely physical.

The "AHA" Moment

While we were writing this book, I was taking a plant medicine facilitator's course through N.A.P.S. (Neuro Alignment Psychedelic System) with our dear friend Todd Ritchey. A requirement of my training was an in-depth examination of my own life event that looked at my past traumas, addictions, judgments, and cultural/family programming.

One of the exercises that I was given was to list past traumas. (Although I've written about it in this book, at that time, I hadn't unlocked the traumas that shaped my persona). I listed my limiting stories, my pain points, and the coping mechanisms that I had adopted. I knew that I was a control freak with sex, I just didn't know why. I had a big blind spot that needed to come to the light.

Josh and I completed some of the exercises together. One day I had an epiphany while we were discussing my desire for control: I was subsumed by the memory of my sexual assault. The gates opened and the memories of my past trauma came flooding in. The lack of control that I felt at sixteen made me feel weak and vulnerable. I had buried it... deep. The burial was driven by the core mechanism of survival.

My solution was to flip the narrative: Consistently, I was the one in control and it rewarded me with a beta-endorphin rush. My choice was to use control as my armor. I wouldn't be a victim again.

"The premise of what I call homeopathic sexuality is founded on the belief that our higher power can guide us to ways to work with our own sexual energy to heal past sexual traumas."
- Barbara Carrellas

That girl was under the influence of an old operating system installed by her parents, her church and her culture. The good girl hadn't found her agency and her right to say "no." Now, I know my no's.

Understanding this life event hasn't changed my approach to sex. I still prefer to be on top sexually, but now I know why. The assault was one of my key life lessons; I needed to go through it. It formed me and made me who I am today.

I like who I am. I admire who I am. I wouldn't change a thing.

An Energetic Experience

It was early one morning and Josh and I were spooning, semi-awake and fully naked. We had no pressing tasks and were enjoying quiet time together. As we were snuggling I could feel Josh's "morning wood" pressing against my ass. I rolled over to give him a good morning kiss and gently touched his erection. I was in the mood and he felt the connection. Our eyes focused on each other, as we synchronized our breath, inhaling and exhaling in the same rhythmic pattern. We brought our awareness into our lower dantian (an energy center located in our pelvic floor region) as we drew our breath into our bellies. I imagined my breath reaching into every nook and cranny of my pelvis.

Josh lightly touched me on my stomach, making circular, ticklish movements with his fingertips. This made my whole body shiver. I closed my eyes as his fingertips moved slowly up to my breasts, igniting my flesh with his touch. As my turn-on intensified, the energy in my lower dantian increased. He circled my breasts with his touch and the tingling sensations amplified. I could feel a clear sensation of energy making its way up my spine.

I took longer inhales with deep exhales, building more energy throughout my entire body. I could sense the movement of life force up through all of my chakras as the Kundalini serpent writhed upwards in response to my breath. Josh moved his hand down to my pelvic mound and pressed the palm of his hand against it. His hand, pulsing with energy, felt hot and stimulating.

My head was swimming in a sea of serotonin. I let out moans of pleasure as I arched my back. I needed to free the energy that was building in my body; I undulated my body, slowly moving my hips and spine to allow the energetic flow of the Kundalini serpent to rise from my pelvic floor up to my crown chakra. As it passed through my throat chakra, I released intense moans of pleasure.

Josh and I were in total sync with each other and I could feel his presence and commitment. I imagined pure white light enveloping us, blanketing our souls while the heat from our passion boiled between us. I opened my eyes to see Josh looking deeply into mine. He kissed me passionately as our energies melded together. I felt a deep closeness to Josh like never before — our minds and bodies were one with each other and it was like we had melded our souls together.

I had never felt such intense pleasure. With our hearts completely open to each other, we melted into each other's embrace. Josh didn't enter me with his cock that day but he penetrated me on a deeper level than I had ever experienced. I silently wished that the feelings could go on forever and in some ways, they have.

There was no money shot to end our connection. To close, we shut our eyes, took a few deep, belly-filling breaths and expressed appreciation for each other. We opened our eyes and enjoyed the expanded experience of intimacy. Just like after a Kundalini exercise, I sat in silence bringing my attention to the sensations cascading throughout my body. I acknowledged and recorded these sensations to my endorphin memory bank for later retrieval.

In the afterglow, we attended to each other's body with care. We felt recharged and energized and openly shared our experience with each other. As always, we were playful, and expressed ourselves through laughter and excitement.

Practicing Tantra has helped me to create a better awareness of my body and a higher level of consciousness. I found that the concept of slowing down and and letting go of the goal of the orgasm was far more pleasurable. I was able to enjoy sex without penetration, something that I never thought would be possible in my Swinger years. I let my mind have the orgasm instead of my pussy. By shifting the focus off the genital orgasm, I was no longer "having sex" or even "making love," I was "making foreplay." The meditation, breath control, body touching and massaging were not a means to an end. Sometimes they are the end. Don't get me wrong, I still like a lot of dick! I just don't need it every time!

Mindgasms

 – *Disclaimer: If this next section is getting too deep, jump to the next one...it's juicy.*

As my understanding of sacred sex grew, so did my understanding of the ways it could be expressed. There were multiple ways for us to reach orgasm including clitoral, G-spot, cervical, anal and stroking. But Josh and I have a new favorite — the mindgasm or energy orgasm.

In many cases, sex is a goal-oriented experience. It heads towards climax for one, preferably both (or all) of the participants. When climax is reached, sex is over. Yet with Tantric practices, unlimited orgasms are possible just by tapping into one's energy system.

We all have this sexual life force energy circulating through our bodies. Mindgasms involve experiencing the sensations of orgasm without the stimulation required for a physical climax. This means no, or very little, physical contact with the genitals. For Josh, these can often be non-ejaculatory orgasms which require no refractory period to recharge. The benefit of this is that he is able to orgasm multiple times during a play session.

Many people only know how to access orgasmic energy when their genitals are being stimulated physically. Some also require a great level of stimulation to achieve this. Difficulties might arise from past traumas, feeling unsafe, physical pain, negative social conditioning, or shame around sexual pleasure. All of these factors and more can affect our belief systems around our sexuality. Our beliefs are foundational to how we experience sex.

People of all genders can learn to orgasm energetically and enjoy the sensation multiple times during a session. I have nearly levitated off the bed as the shared energy coursed through my body from head to toe. No direct stimulation is required. I find through breathing, mindfulness and awareness, I can access orgasmic sensations from my memory bank at will.

The sensations and feelings that come over my body during an energy orgasm are varied. They can shift, depending on the partner I am playing with and they can even differ, depending on the day, when Josh and I are together. Experimentation is key and Josh and I have had plenty of enjoyable practice to find the ways that work best for us to achieve the satisfaction of mindgasm. From our personal experience, we have developed the following practice to attain energetic expansion and flow:

1. We find a quiet time, free from interruptions. All beeps and buzzers turned off.

2. We wear soft, loose comfortable clothing or none at all.

3. Our room is quiet and warm, with minimal distractions.

4. We begin by laying comfortably on our backs, knees bent and feet flat on the floor. We ensure our spines are straight and we don't use a pillow.

5. We turn our attention inward, closing our eyes to signal our mind that it's time to relax and let go. Trying too hard can create blocks in the practice.

6. We start with the BREATH, by breathing deeply into our pelvic floor/root chakra. We imagine our breath stoking the fires of our arousal. As with yoga, the breath is the most important element of the practice.

7. We lift our hips to our breath and melt any tension in our body.

8. By focusing our attention to the area around our genitals, we connect to our eroticism. Sometimes having one of us place a hand on my pelvic mound during this time helps amplify the energy and helps me to stay present and focused on my lower dantian. (The lower dantian is believed by some to be the seat of life force energy in the body). I can also do this practice alone and get amazing results.

9. Kegels - We squeeze our pelvic floor muscles on the inhale breath as we visualize drawing the sexual energy up through our spines.

10. Once we feel the warmth beginning to move up our spines, we touch our tongue to the palate of our mouths and imagine it circulating back down to our genitals and back up again. We sometimes use our hands to help conduct the energy, moving it up the spine and down again. The contact point on the skin helps to maintain focus.

11. As the orgasmic fire is stoked within our bodies, we allow the *sounds* of pleasure to be heard. Making orgasmic sounds helps to release stuck energies and opens pathways for them to flow. Pleasure sounds are also arousing for both of us. The pitch of our sounds often increases as we move the energy up our spine.

12. *Movement* keeps things flowing. We allow our bodies to rise up with the energies and breath. Undulating the hips helps me to visualize and feel the arousal flowing through my body. It also helps release the vagus nerve, allowing the sacred connection between hips and heart.

13. Keep with the *breath*. We let ourselves go, without being self-conscious. We continue to *breathe* fully.

14. Now, let it roll. We stay present with it as long as we desire. We ride the wave.

Josh and I may get distracted during the practice or have days when we feel less energized. That is normal. Our energy levels rise and fall from day to day and even within each day. We refocus by returning to the base chakra and pulling the energy to the area we want energized. By the end of the practice, we always feel revitalized.

As we have grown older, our bodies' pace has slowed but our minds remain alert. We no longer fuck like bunnies. Mindgasms have been an excellent evolution in our intimate physical relationships.

You're Not the Boss of Me!

Josh and I were excited to attend a Tantra festival. We didn't know what to expect so when we pulled our RV into our camping spot and saw Travis, I knew the weekend was off to a good start. Yay for hot neighbors!

Travis was a striking man with a shaved head, goatee, and strong, tall body. He was our neighbor for the weekend with his Westfalia parked next to our Tantra Shala. I introduced myself and invited him to join us later that evening to chat and get to know one another. He turned me on and immediately, I could feel my clit getting hard and tingly.

Our evening together was filled with stimulating conversation. Travis worked as a couples counselor and Josh and I shared our experience living in an open relationship. He was keen to know how we happily navigated non-monogamy for the past twenty years, especially considering many of his clients have challenges with monogamy.

Tucked into the marriage contract is the idea of "forsaking all others" and Josh and I were excitedly inviting others into our connection. Our relationship is based on honesty and we would never "cheat" behind each other's back when we derive so much enjoyment from shared pleasure and compersion. We respect and trust each other enough to be truthful about our desires and fantasies and we know that there will always be a Josh and Maggie.

After a few hours of stimulating conversation, it was getting late and we said goodbye for the night. Travis had brought some topics into the light and we had a lot to think about. His interest in our marriage was another call to write this book. It motivated us to reflect on our Lifestyle and helped us understand that we had something special to share with others.

The following day we all attended Tantric workshops on sensual and energetic exploration. We learned about using authentic communication to express our boundaries, fears and desires, something not discussed at Lifestyle events. Since then, we've adopted these as part of our protocol before engaging in play.

Throughout the day, every time I saw Travis, I could feel the sexual energy arise in me and I could sense he was feeling the same. At the end of the day, we invited him back to our motorhome to explore some of our newfound knowledge.

I got aroused as Josh and I took a shower and spent a few minutes together before Travis arrived. We were connected and we could feel our erotic energies increasing in anticipation of whatever would unfold during the night ahead. Our openness to new possibilities was exhilarating.

Josh set up our cuddle puddle and prepared our space. Meanwhile, I prepared myself: I brushed my hair, put on some glossy hot pink lipstick, and slipped on a silky, red kimono. With the knock on the door, my whole body fluttered. I swung the door open and there stood Travis with a sexy grin on his face. Damn. He looked good enough to eat.

I could see him looking at my breasts as my kimono slipped slightly open. Oops! Sorry, not sorry. An erotic feeling unlocked inside me, it was something freeing - I felt unleashed and I was ravenous to feel him. Every encounter has always been so entirely unique. *That* is what turns me on.

We all sat on the floor on the soft blankets. I wanted to be in control so after holding myself back from devouring Travis, I asked him to kiss my pussy. I reclined on my back with my knees up. He lay on his stomach with his shoulders under my thighs and gazed at the vulva between my legs. He kissed the inside of my right thigh and then sucked the inside of my left. My juices were flowing and he tasted them with his tongue.

I could feel the sexual energy rise within me. Taking control, he wrapped his arms around my legs and buried his head between my thighs. My breath deepened as the energy pulsed throughout my body. He pushed my legs up and further apart as his eyes connected with mine. I felt his warm breath wash over my pussy, as he hovered his mouth over my swollen lips. "More," I gasped to Trevor as I kissed Josh hungrily.

I had never known another man, aside from Josh, who was so hungry for my pussy. He flattened his tongue against my oversensitive clit and trailed it back and forth in long, slow strokes. My body felt alive and fully charged as a shock of pleasure vibrated through my system. Every cell in my body was titillated. I was completely at ease with him and totally turned on.

I looked over at Josh and kissed him. This sent a twinge of energy up my spine. Josh's body jolted with pleasure as he sucked softly on my lips. "More," I gasped again as I kissed him hungrily. Another bolt of energy shot up my spine. I could feel my body pulsing and the energy rising as I came to a full mindgasm. My eyes rolled back as I surrendered to pleasure.

Josh and I locked eyes. We took a few deep breaths to slow things down. I leaned forward and turned my attention to Travis. We kissed as our tongues wrestled, playfully vying for dominance. I wanted to taste all of him so I directed my tongue down his chest and onto his hard nipples. He responded with moans of pleasure. I licked a line down his body, finally engulfing his rock hard cock in my mouth. I used one hand to gently massage his balls. He raised his hips slightly accepting my touch.

In that moment, I recalled the tantric workshop topic of "Boundaries, Fears, and Desires" from earlier that day. I felt so at ease with Travis that I had the space to confront one of my fears...my teenage sexual trauma. I looked into Travis' eyes and said, "I need to express my boundaries, fears and desires." I continued, "I don't want you to put your hands on my head and I don't like to have my head pushed down on any man's penis. My desire is to enjoy this moment with me in control." There. I was in a situation that had the potential to trigger me yet I used my big girl voice. It felt good.

Travis replied, "I understand and thank you for sharing your feelings." He was completely respectful and willing to engage with me however I showed up. I was good to go. But then...

I mentally paused for a moment and said, "On second thought, I *would* like you to put your hands on my head and push my head down as I suck your cock." I wasn't going to be a victim of that past experience anymore. It was time for me to challenge myself and confront those fears. It was time for me to break free.

Travis smiled and nodded. He was the willing stranger who would help me shift my mindset. As he lay on the blanket, I hovered above him on all fours. I teased and stroked his shaft while looking directly into his eyes. He shivered as I licked his crown ridge with my tongue. We maintained our gaze and I could see and hear his pleasure.

Then I took the tip of his cock, sucking it with my lips. Travis held the back of my head, gently pushing his erection deep into my mouth. In and out. I gagged for a second. I put my hand on his hand and he released the pressure from my head.

This was a new beginning for me. I was going to let go of the past and bring all of my energy into that present moment.

I turned and smiled at Josh. He had positioned himself behind me and I wanted him inside my pussy. My juices were flowing and his hard cock easily penetrated my warmth. The more he thrust, the more I took Travis deeply into my mouth. I allowed him to firmly force my head onto his cock. It was both exciting and scary.

I was bookended with cocks. I could feel their desire and how much they both wanted to give me pleasure. My skin was electrified from head to toe. The waves of energy rose within me, crashing like a tidal wave. I cried out as I was cumming. It was the cry of a free woman and it rocked me to the core. I laid back on the blanket with a smile on my face. I was free. Courage and pleasure had helped set me free.

For years I never enjoyed giving BJs. They were a "job" and definitely felt like work to me. I did them to be giving and to reciprocate, but I never really enjoyed them. I did enjoy that with kissing, sucking and stroking, I could get most men's cocks hard and ready for some pounding. But I would never swallow. Nor would I let a man push down on my head. I wanted to be in control. But, I was not. That old story still held me in its grip.

Life was there to support me. The tantric workshop had given me the tools to express my fears freely. Travis was a willing and empathetic stranger who played a role in my story. In that instance, I decided that I wasn't going to let the story determine how I enjoyed my life. To be the true Mistress of my own experience, I needed to relinquish my need to control. I had to surrender to the experience to reclaim it. By doing my personal work, I took the work out of blowjob and was well on my way to considering them play. In my mind, I have re-phrased the word "blowjob" to "blobby." Now, I think of it as a hobby.

Josh - I knew in my heart that something was different that night. Maggie was excited about the playdate she had arranged with Travis. We don't often find ourselves with single, straight men but there we were, naked in our little "cuddle puddle."

It was different for me not to have physical contact with our third. I took a back seat to the action as Maggie instructed her new lover on ways he could satisfy her cravings. I cradled her as Travis savored her pussy, taking his time to raise her arousal.

Maggie and I kissed deeply and I felt her body shudder with pleasure. Her eyes looked deeply into mine. I could feel her love and her appreciation of his attention but now it was her turn to give. She asked Travis to recline as she turned her attention to his rigid cock. I sat back on the sofa which gave me a perfect view of her long, blonde hair draping over his body, her fine ass in the air. What a view!

She worshipped his cock with long licks and kisses. Then she spoke to him, but her words were unclear. I assumed it was about his desires and preferences but when I saw him place his hands on her head, I realized it was about her fears. I knew she didn't enjoy having anyone's hand on her head but there she was, embracing it. I entered protector mode but soon realized that she was in full control.

A few minutes later, she raised her head and looked at me with an invitation to enter her from behind, which I quickly did. I held her hips as she rocked back and forth, alternately consuming my cock in her pussy and Travis' in her mouth. The momentum built until I blew my load, filling her with my juices.

It wasn't until afterwards that Maggie gave me the details of her experience. I was unaware of the courageous dance she had just performed with her demon, but I was happy that she was the one leading.

Playing with Fyre

It was a Sunday afternoon and Josh and I were invited to a beautiful mansion for a Self Care Day. The hosts were three colorful gender-queer and trans folks. Our lifestyle is outside the norm and we are comfortable with others living counter to mainstream culture so we felt excited to explore. We were also intrigued because we knew that the basement of the mansion had a fully equipped (sex) dungeon.

The twelve of us in attendance began the afternoon sitting on the living room floor in a circle. As we each took turns holding a talking stick, we shared how we would like to spend the afternoon giving and receiving care and pleasure. Some wanted to give full-body massages, while others wanted to spend time in the sauna and cold baths. When it was my turn to talk, I knew exactly what I wanted...I wanted to be tied down to the hard-points on the bondage table in the dungeon. For years, I was the dominant one and wanted to be in control of my playtime with others. I wanted to shift that dynamic and somehow, in a room filled with strangers, I took the opportunity to create the experience of being submissive.

After the circle, I was approached by Raynefyre, an Erotic Breath and Body Worker who was experienced in Fire Play. (As a gender queer person, they use neutral pronouns they/them/their.) They offered to be my Dominant and grant my desire. After I was tied down, they would perform their Fire Play ritual with me. Although it seemed slightly risky, it sounded exciting. They were strikingly attractive to me so I was in.

To make me feel comfortable, they gave me a quick demonstration of Fire Play by lighting my arm on fire and quickly extinguishing the flame with their hand. I could smell the burnt hair on my arm, but instead of being afraid, I was tantalized. After our negotiation, Raynefyre and I climbed onto the black leather bondage table, sat cross-legged and held hands. We eye-gazed, breathing and joining our energies together. My anticipation grew as others sat around the room to watch the performance. I always enjoyed an audience.

I could feel Raynefyre's kind and caring vibes filling me. I took off my bra an panties and lay face up on the pool table. After tying my hair back, Raynefyre put wrist and ankle straps on to restrain me. They clipped me into the rings on the table, each time making sure that I was comfortable. With my arms and legs spread wide, I was now completely naked, fully exposed and attached to the corners of the table. What had I signed up for?

When they blindfolded my eyes, I began taking long, deep breaths and could feel my body relaxing with each exhale. Raynefyre pressed both of their hands on my chest and I reacted with a twinge as an electrical shock passed through my whole body. I could feel their energy going deep into my being.

Next, I felt the warm flame from the burning firesticks as they traveled just above my skin, flowing from my neck down to my toes and then back again. When those flames died, Raynefyre dipped one stick into an alcohol mixture while the other remained lit as a constant source of ignition. The cooling liquid was applied to my skin in a circular motion and almost immediately, I felt the warm feeling that I knew was the flame burning on my flesh. Just as quickly as the fire would spread across my skin, Raynefyre would brush their hand over the flame, smothering it before it could damage my flesh.

Raynefyre traced my upper body, my chest, breasts and belly, then made their way to my pelvic mound. When they spread the alcohol on my pussy, tingles spread throughout the area. I was exhilarated as I waited in anticipation for the fire. I was steeped in pleasure.

Using the sticks, RF fire-drummed all over my naked body. The music they chose was mesmerizing and their drumming continued to the beat. Each time the fire sticks hit my body, I felt the heat and it jolted me. My arousal was building.

I felt the pleasure chemicals rising up my body. RF repeated into my ear, "Concentrate on your breath." As I focused on my breathing, I reached a meditative state of consciousness. The drumming stopped and I asked Raynefyre to lay on me and press their shirtless chest onto mine. Fully embracing me with their loving presence, I could feel our bodies' energies flowing together. Despite being tied down, I undulated my back and hips. I so wanted to wrap my arms around their strong body.

My pubic bone was rubbing up against their semi-hard packing cock (although their cock wasn't like anything I had ever experienced, they embodied it and I was completely turned on). I then said, "Kiss me." We locked lips and tongues together and my body shook as tingles shot up my spine. The ecstasy of both pain and pleasure came together, exploding in my body and my mind in a full-mind and body orgasm.

I was beginning to sense a change in my play style. I felt a yearning for more intimate and sensual playtime with others. My intentions were beginning to change. I wanted to experience more kink!

Josh - At times, playing with fire is exactly the right thing to do on a Sunday afternoon. Maggie had chosen to be the receiver of Fire Play from Raynefyre, an experienced erotic arts practitioner. I was exhilarated to watch the scene unfold. I stared as Raynefyre traced Maggie's body with the flaming sticks, equally concerned as I was aroused.

By this time in our relationship, we were both skilled at compersion. I enjoyed observing Maggie, rising to the pleasure. It thrilled me to see her being watched and appreciated by the other guests in the room. Every time her body would ride an orgasmic wave it brought a smile to my face and it stirred me to an erection. I felt part of the scene.

Maggie had requested that I record the Fire Play for her to view later - her own private erotic video. Looking through the lens at her receiving such pleasure and recording the scene was a task that I loved. Another one for our spank bank.

Sacred Sexuality

Sex has been many things to us throughout our lives. On some occasions, it was a very selfish act of personal gratification. At other times, it was an act of transactional gratification — "You scratch my back and I'll scratch yours." Some sexual practices were learned through porn which sometimes led to objectifying the act and the people involved. Sex was frequently experienced as conquest based. These approaches almost always produced an orgasm, but they were often short and unfulfilling. Through our Swinger years, we experienced all of these interpretations of sex. This all shifted after our plant medicine journeys when we realized that, "We are not a body, we have a body." Enter... sacred sexuality.

Sacred sexuality is completely contrary to what our culture presents as the typical experience of sex. Through the media, we are frequently exposed to sex as externally focused and goal oriented. These portrayals may influence how we experience sex and take us away from being present, focused, and journey-oriented. They influenced me until I experienced another way.

When Josh and I began our Neo-Tantric practice, it opened up energies that we never knew existed. It allowed us to be more present. Our sex life has become more deeply intimate, even when it involves other people. It has been a change from bodies clashing to bodies, minds, hearts, and energies dancing.

I had thought that my sex life was amazing but I never knew that there was more pleasure to be found. I now understand that sex is transformational and life-changing. When I added all the multi-layered elements of who I am to the sexual experience, it shifted from being physically gratifying to being gratifying mentally, emotionally, and dare I say it...spiritually. Sex has become a pleasure dance with the Divine. If it was hot before, it is white hot now. It is still sexy as fuck.

> *"Sexuality is one of the ways that we become enlightened, actually, because it leads us to self-knowledge."*
> - Alice Walker

Discovering the Divine Energies

No matter what our gender is, we are all a mixture of both masculine and feminine energies. In Asian culture, this is expressed as Yin and Yang, two interconnected yet opposing forces. In Hinduism, these forces are seen through the god Shiva, and the goddess Shakti. Regardless of the lens of interpretation, we are each a mixture of the divine feminine and masculine energies and it can be fun to play with our under expressed sides.

Josh has always been in touch with his feminine side. As with most children of our generation, his loving mother was his primary care-giver. While his dad focused on his business and worked hard at providing for the family, it was his mom who supported Josh at most of his sporting events and hobbies. This helped develop his feminine energy. He has the ability to discern when to present his masculine side and when to express his feminine side.

The natural match for Josh's softer, feminine side was my masculine, powerhouse energy. As mentioned, I never showed my dominant side to him when we were intimate because I wanted him to be dominant in bed. I only showed my vulnerability to Josh, not to other men. When we started in the Lifestyle, I was excited to freely express my dominant masculine energy. I was assertive and confident and expressed my desires freely. I was the driving force that flirted and set up dates with the other couples. I came on strong with the men and I could tell that the men liked it.

On the other hand, Josh had a softer, feminine approach. He sat back and allowed the evening to progress without his direct control. He would have a listening ear and would let a woman come to him on her own terms. When she did, he would worship her pussy. He could spend hours between a woman's legs just enveloped in her lady parts. He always kept in the moment and made his partner feel like a goddess. When he surrendered to my masculine energy and allowed me to fuck him, he embraced the feminine energy of receptiveness. We have it all within us and it can be extremely sexy to explore it all.

Josh and I were a power couple. The balance of the feminine and masculine energy was fluid in us. I used my strong masculine energy to get the man I wanted and Josh used his soft feminine energy to gain the trust of the woman he wanted. Our life story together has always been a dance between the masculine side for control and the feminine side for nurturing and affection.

My journey has allowed me to understand that although I present as female and was born into a female body, I am a combination of the divine masculine and the divine feminine energies. When these are in balance, I have the ability to express both sides of myself, I have more balance in my life and more union with the environment around me.

Connecting to My Sacred Sexuality

Once I became aware of the divine energies, I embraced them, and my life changed. Sex went from "Wham Bam..." to a sexual practice. Josh and I attracted different playmates, mostly single women, who would open themselves up to us. They wanted to discover more about themselves and understand our new energetic sexual play. Random conversations would often migrate towards sexuality. Their curiosity was evident and we loved to share.

As French philosopher, Pierre Teilhard de Chardin, wrote, "We are not human beings having a spiritual experience; we are spiritual beings having a human experience." At the core of our journey was the shift from our bodies getting sexual gratification to becoming spiritual beings sharing pleasure and intimacy through our bodies.

Some things have not changed: Sex is still fulfilling, natural, erotic and fun! What has changed is how we have sex. Now, Josh and I set time aside which allows us to savor the moment. We still enjoy the occasional "quickie" but it's more like fast food, filling the body but not nourishing it. We embrace the act of sex as a form of worship. Sex is recognized as part of our spirituality. When we recognize the Divine in our partners, they recognize the Divine in themselves and in us. We are sacred mirrors for each other.

Josh and I create a space together that encourages sacred sex. Sound, smell, and touch are all facets of this experience. Just like with many ceremonies, we light candles. We choose music that is not too loud or wordy and we keep the lighting low. A warm room helps keep the obstructions of clothing to a minimum. This makes the vibe comfortable.

When seeking the Divine, it helps to have a clean temple. This means preparing our bodies: We trim, shave, pluck, do our hair, and do whatever makes us feel our best.

We frequently start by sitting very close and eye-gazing. We then connect through circular breathing: one of us inhales while the other exhales and vice versa. Breath creates a flow of energy between us and connects us emotionally. It brings us both into the present moment. Being fully in the moment during sex means having total awareness of our being and the sensations and emotions that we share. We immerse ourselves in the experience.

When we are in the present moment, we follow the energy and our sexual intuition. When thoughts of the past and the future are gone, new inspirations can arise that allow for new ways to explore our partner's body and give him/her pleasure. We may apply essential oils to each other's soft, bare skin to release any tension if that is needed in the moment. We may focus on making out. We may express a new fantasy or desire which we listen to without judgment and with the excitement of possibility. What we don't do is follow a sexual script.

Sex occurs freely when we are mutually consenting adults, playing within the boundaries of our comfort zone. There need not be feelings of guilt or embarrassment. By embracing sex as a form of worship of our partner, we are honoring him/her as a sacred representation of the Divine.

A few of our female playmates had some experience in the Lifestyle but for others, it was all new. We openly discussed the Lifestyle, our relationship, and our newfound understanding of what sex could be. Many found that expressing themselves without fear of judgment helped them explore their true sexual beings.

The old hetero-normative approach wasn't working for our play partners, nor for us. The traditional male/female power dynamics got in the way of embracing sexual freedom. They were discovering themselves and the pleasures that they could enjoy by releasing their inhibitions and accepting the attention they were being offered. We also helped them voice their boundaries and express their desires and fears. Expressing both strength and vulnerability allowed for more intimacy.

Occasionally, a playmate might grant themselves permission at the moment but in hindsight second-guess their decision. When this happened, we found that guilt and shame were often at the core. Pleasure has often been equated with sin, as was the case in our religious youth. We have broken free from this old paradigm but many are still in its clutches. Toxic sex-shaming messages have taken a heavy toll on our sexual identities. Sexual shame can stand in the way of confidence, intimacy, establishing healthy relationships with partners, sex, and self-pleasure. The God of my understanding is all about pleasure.

Happy Customers

It has been rewarding to know the impact that Josh and I have had on many of our playmates. A good example of this is Charlene and Jack, experienced Lifestylers who came over one night wanting to learn about our new approach to playtime.

It didn't take long for us to get settled into our Zen Den and get naked. Charlene's desire was to experience a deeper, energetic sexual encounter. Jack's desire that night was to observe, learn and immerse himself in her pleasure. I admired the compersion that he had for her; it was a real turn-on.

Excited to be voyeurs, Jack and I cuddled on the bed and watched the scene unfold. Ensuring that our view wasn't blocked, Josh positioned himself on the far side of Charlene who reclined on her back next to us.

Josh and Charlene locked eyes and connected, being totally present with each other. Allowing the ambient music to set the pace, they breathed deeply and in sync. I quietly narrated the scene to make Jack comfortable and open to what he was witnessing.

Josh caressed Charlene's neck, shoulders and hair adding a hair-pulling technique that I taught him. He lightly caressed her body, sending tingles of anticipation along her skin. His hands glided over her large breasts and gently stroked her nipples to erection. Moving his hands over her smooth belly, he teased his way past her pussy and proceeded to her feet.

With a big grin on his face, Josh reached over to the nightstand and scooped out a generous portion of coconut oil. Rubbing his hands together, he warmed the oil. When he started on Charlene's feet, chills of excitement ran up my spine. Feet are one of my favorite erogenous zones.

I could see Charlene's face light up as Josh massaged his way up her legs and into her inner thighs. Her breath quickened as his hand gently cupped her mound. Her anticipation was building. My narration to Jack was arousing me, building the sexual energy in my body.

Josh inserted his thumb into Charlene's pussy and pressed his hand firmly against her labia. Focusing all of his energy on her root, he held still while she took long, deep breaths. I knew she was feeling the warmth radiate into her base chakra. He pressed firmly against her pelvic bone, awakening her clit. When he does it to me, his thumb hits my G-spot perfectly and the feeling of his hand over my folds drives me crazy. Based on her sounds of pleasure, I knew Charlene was feeling the same.

Josh alternated between vibrating the palm of his hand on her mound and holding still, giving space to the turn-on. Jack and I watched as Josh massaged her breasts. He then placed his hand on her heart and felt the rise and fall of her breath. They both shuddered with random bursts of orgasmic energy. Finally, Charlene's hips rose skyward as she surrendered to the energy as it rode up her spine. The look on her face and the sounds she was expressing was erotic as fuck.

To say, "You had to be there" is a cheat yet this wasn't the regular type of sex scene. When sex is purely physical, the action can be described and frequently, the description can be a turn-on. Here, the turn-on was largely energetic and not based entirely on putting (sensitive) objects in (sensitive) holes. What I can relate is that even from the sidelines, our turn-on was palpable. And Jack had the erection to prove it.

The next day, our informal Yelp review from Jack and Charlene was that the experience had changed their approach to love-making.

> *Bringing breath and energy awareness*
> *into play adds an entirely new dimension of desire.*
> *This practice has become intoxicating, to say the least*
> *- Charlene*

One day in Paris

Paris was curvaceous blonde with wavy hair, a beautiful smile and blue eyes. She was a stunning woman, a few years younger than me. We were introduced when a mutual friend of ours brought her to one of our Lifestyle parties.

Paris knew that Josh and I experienced journeys with ayahuasca, mushrooms and cannabis so she reached out to me. A few weeks later, I invited her over for afternoon tea so we could talk and could give her an Akashic Reading. From that afternoon, she started coming over for weekly visits. Soon she shared that she was having sexual desires for me. Oh, I found that very titillating!

I hadn't been with many other females and it was usually in the situation of another couple. I really enjoyed the connection of kissing and caressing another woman while the men looked at us with lust in their eyes. At that time, I really wasn't into going down on a woman — I tried it on a few occasions, but never truly got into it. I did, however, always love to touch women's breasts and kiss their soft, sensual lips. That was a real turn-on.

I fantasized about Paris' yearning for me. It was titillating and arousing to think about the possibilities. I talked to Josh about inviting her over for a playdate, just to see what would happen. We both had adopted a "Go with the flow, no pressure" approach. So I called Paris and arranged a playdate.

It was 3 pm and Paris came over wearing a tight, knit top and skinny jeans. Josh and I both complimented her on how hot she looked. I poured us a cup of kombucha and we sat down to chat. It didn't take long until we were all upstairs in our Zen Den.

The three of us were quick to strip off our clothes and tangle our naked bodies together on the bed. We already had weeks of mental foreplay since Paris expressed her feelings to me so we jumped right in. I kissed her soft, sensual lips, as she ran her fingers through my hair and then kissed my neck. This turned me on, big time.

Josh was positioned on the other side of Paris and watched us intently; he loved to see me giving and receiving pleasure. I reached over and touched his arm and made eye contact with him. It felt good for me to connect with him in the midst of my arousal.

Paris was excited and expressed how much she was enjoying her time with us. We reassured her that the feelings were mutual and then we devoured our little Unicorn: we kissed, fondled, and caressed every inch of her. She lay back and surrendered, moaning with pleasure.

Before too long, Paris excused herself from our embrace and got up to pull a Feeldoe out of her bag. Playfully, she looked me in the eyes as she said she wanted to fuck me with the double-sided dildo. That sounded like a fantastic idea to me — I love a creative playmate! She reclined on the bed and sensually inserted one end of the dildo into her waiting pussy, while the other end stood up like a raging hard-on.

I covered the head with lube and climbed on top. Looking into each others eyes, I slowly inserted the big black cock into my waiting pussy. My juices added to the lubrication and it slid into me with ease. I sat on top of her body grinding and thrusting my hips and each time I rocked, her breasts shook in waves.

I leaned forward and we locked lips, our wet tongues tasting each other's juices. I taunted her nipples and toyed with her full, pillowy breasts. Our breathing increased and soon her thrusting and my grinding brought us to climax. But that wasn't enough...she told me that once she came, she could cum multiple times. She had no limit to pleasure, but neither did I. It became a game of laughter and delight as we explored how many times we could make each other climax.

Well before we were spent, we turned our attention to Josh who was patiently watching and waiting for his invitation. We pounced on him, dominating him with our desires. I queened him by sitting on his face, my pussy nestled onto his full lips as his tongue moved across my clit. I turned my head to see Paris on all fours, kneeling in front of Josh and giving him a deep-throated blow job. Fuck I loved watching Josh get pleasured! It made me so turned on.

It was an evening of gratification in our new Zen Den. At times, Josh and I would take breaks and just cuddle with our Unicorn between us. I would reach over and stroke his leg and kiss him on his lips. The connection would send us both into a full energetic body orgasm or mindgasm.

Since that night, Paris has come for kombucha on several occasions. Our playtime together has become a special time for all three of us.

Finding someone that enhances our sex lives in such a compatible way has added a wonderfully sexy dynamic to our relationship and her life as well.

Josh - The evening started with a light dinner. Maggie and I enjoyed getting to know Paris over a glass of Maggie's homemade kombucha. We enjoyed Paris' energy in our space and we shared common interests in plant medicines and spirituality. The topics eventually led to Tantric sex and energy sharing and how we incorporated it into our sexual practice.

From there, we moved the discussion into our Zen Den. We lay together on the bed and allowed the energies of arousal to build. Our clothes slowly came off as we explored each other's bodies with sensual touching. I gently whispered into Paris' ear, asking her if it was OK to touch her. She responded with a reassuring, "Yes."

As I traced her body with my fingertips, I felt my own body tingle with excitement. I could sense the sexual energy in my body and I was vibrating with it. It was like my fascia was a conduit for this electricity to travel through every limb.

One of my biggest turn-ons is watching a woman pleasure herself in front of me, and this evening didn't disappoint. Paris went deep within herself as she used a vibrator to bring herself to a climax in front of us. It was a magical evening full of laughter, sensuality, self-discovery and orgasms. We gained a new and playful friend.

> *"The relationship that I have with Maggie and Josh is a supportive and luscious connection that helps all of us grow spiritually into more loving humans. It's sensual, completely unique, balanced, loving, fun, playful and soulful"*
> - Paris

Consenting Adults

When Josh and I started in the Lifestyle, the rules around consent were very clear. Swingers made the decision to attend the events while of sound mind, knowing and desiring the evenings to turn sexy. When the evening did turn sexy, the rules of engagement were discussed by the women beforehand, then it was game on.

When we embarked on our new sexplorations, these were mostly away from the Swinger framework, and we soon realized that we would have to create our own good practices for engagement. One  of these turned into our Rule Number 7 - always obtain consent before consuming mind-altering substances. This includes alcohol and drugs of any kind. The decision to play should always be made when sober. We frequently have this discussion over my delicious homemade kombucha.

Even when someone expresses desire before coming over to our Zen Den, we now have a conversation around consent before taking anything that may alter his/her inhibitions. Included in this conversation is asking if our playmate has any personal boundaries or fears/concerns around playing together. Once these are understood, the conversation can turn to desires. When all the rules of engagement are understood...let the games begin!

Embodied Sexuality

Josh and I call our RV our mobile Zen Den. We like to park it in our favorite camping spot — a tranquil, forested area on a small island one hour from our house. On the dining room wall, there is a tapestry of the Tree Of Life. A mushroom fantasy wall tapestry covers a 6-foot area in the bedroom. The strip lighting under the counter tops brings a soft red glow to the space. Our "cuddle puddle" is an area on the carpeted floor that we set up with large fluffy blankets and dozens of pillows. Confession...we are nouveau Hippies!

A typical evening begins with soft trance music playing throughout the motor home. We dim the lights and burn incense to fill the space with an aroma of mystique. Candles are scattered around to create a warm glow. We usually invite a couple or a single to join us for an evening of "glamping" and exploration of Neo-Tantra energy sharing.

As mentioned previously, our friend Raynefyre is an Erotic Breath and Body Worker and we were excited to share our love bus with them. (They identify as gender queer and use the pronouns they/them) Josh and I greeted them with a tight embrace and a deep passionate kiss on their lips when they arrived. I could feel the sexual tension rising between us instantly as my body let out a little flutter of energy. Almost immediately, we sat in our cuddle puddle and got comfortable. The conversation was light and the tensions and stress of our daily routines began to slip away as we got into the flow of the evening.

Josh and I have learned not to plan ahead; we never know if we are going to have an evening of cuddling, a night of kink play, or hours of deep-diving into conversations about non-duality and spiritualism. We just go with the flow. We've let go of expectations so there are never any disappointments. That night, however, our clothes came off quickly and Raynefyre and I sat across from each other in easy pose on the floor and held hands. We gazed into each other's eyes and our energies merged. I felt the love in the safe space that Josh and I had created. I could feel Josh's energetic presence beside us as he held space for us. We talked about our boundaries, fears and desires.

That night with Raynefyre, I entered new territory. Josh and I discovered that for Raynefyre, being gender queer means that they have a hybrid body with a vulva and a surgically altered masculine chest. I was intrigued and I felt the desire to explore them completely. I gathered my yearning and whispered into their ear, "Can I lick your pussy?" They said "Yes!" My heart raced at the thought. I kissed their strong chest and stomach and traced their firm, toned body with my lips. And then I was at their labia...I spread their smooth soft, pink lips with my fingers as I looked up into their eyes. I could taste and smell their readiness as I enveloped their vulva with my mouth.

I looked over to Josh who was sitting next to Raynefyre. He responded with a little smirk. I felt something different inside of me...I was not in my body... I was not the physical body licking their pussy...I was imagining that I was Josh and it was his lips and tongue on their opening. I devoured Raynefyre's throbbing clit, licking harder, faster and then deeper into their juicy folds. It was like I was channeling Josh when he buries his head deep into *my* pussy. I moaned and groaned and felt the energy going through my whole body as the Kundalini inside me rose up my spine. A surge of inner strength filled my body as I continued to suck on their deliciousness. My body was rolling in ecstasy. It was like I knew and felt everything that Josh would have felt — his pure love tenderness, compassion, joy, and excitement. I was having a full-on mindgasm. My body tingled and twitched as the power flowed up and through my body. I moved back up to kiss Raynefyre, sharing their own sexy juices that were smeared all over my lips.

I felt a strong connection between all of us. It was like I was an avatar for Josh as he sat by the sidelines, thoroughly turned on by my actions. I was embodying my divine masculine: the assertive and confident conquerer. It was Josh's turn to take an active role in our union...

Josh - Raynefyre and I sat facing each other, holding hands and staring into each other's eyes until we were present and focused on each other. Their healed top surgery scars were evident on their strong chest. I was in a completely new arena...people with pussies in the Lifestyle world were only ever getting enhancements, not breast removal. This beautiful human was new to me in every way and I wanted to explore more.

Raynefyre expressed a desire to straddle me in a cowboy position and I happily agreed. My penis was already hard when they lowered themselves onto me, spreading their swollen labia to envelope my shaft. They didn't insert me, they just wrapped their soft lips around my cock and, slowly, slid themselves down my shaft. My penis remained erect and on the outside of their luscious lips.

Our eyes locked. I could feel their sexual juices lubricating our connection as they moved up and down my cock. Raynefyre confidently brought their knowledge of cock pleasuring to a professional level. They stroked my shaft with their hands and massaged my balls and surrounding areas. I could see the pleasure that it was bringing them — it was like they had taken possession of my penis and they were experiencing it as if it were their own. Visually, the way it extended out from their groin, it looked like it was their cock. They stroked my shaft like they were masturbating their own penis. It was a total sexual embodiment for me. My energy had merged with Raynefyre and it felt like we were one. I had access to all of the sensations that they were feeling, plus my own. It was won-

*derfully confusing for me, not knowing whether to focus on their fantasy
or my own enjoyment. I was the actor on both sides of the scene, the giver
and the receiver.*

*Raynefyre brought themselves to orgasm as they stroked my cock. I had
my own energy orgasm as I watched them cum. Our special connection
gave me insight into another level of sacred sexual play. I am a lifetime
learner of sexual pleasure. I enjoy how my world is forever expanding.*

The Madonna/Whore Schism

Not many women get to adulthood without some kind of sexual or
emotional trauma. My story with my first boss puts me in the majority. It's like I was groomed for it with phrases such as:
"Be a good girl and play well with others."
"Respect your elders."
"Don't make a scene."
"No need to talk about it — it wasn't that violent."
I wasn't sure of what was acceptable behavior because what I was
told didn't always match what I felt inside. I was told to listen and
obey, so I most frequently did. I had a choice to be the good girl or
the bad girl (The Madonna or the Whore). I mostly chose the good
girl.

When the situation happened with my boss, I wondered if I was responsible. Did I lead him on? I buried the experience deep into my
psyche because I had no idea how to correct it. I didn't have the tools
or the resources to know how to deal with it. By choosing well, I selected Josh as my partner, someone who didn't reinforce my trauma
but treated me with the love and respect that I always deserved.

With age came the understanding that the treatment I received from
my boss wasn't acceptable. Through my Lifestyle years, I learned to
manage my fears and desires (healing can come in unexpected packages). Our culture says we should not talk about our sexual pleasure.
Women, and especially ladies, should be reserved and prudish. This
paradigm was an obstacle to accessing my pleasure. However, the
more I talked about what I wanted and needed, the more naturally
my desires could be expressed. If anything, that's what I'd want my

sixteen year-old self to know, "Ask for what you want. Say no to what you don't want."

In our early years of Swinging, Josh was instrumental in helping me learn to express my desires freely. He had an allowance for all of me and I could openly and honestly communicate with him. As I shared my fantasies, it brought us closer. My fantasies were normalized and sharing them brought them into the light so I could enact almost all of them. A life where fantasies and reality coincide is a great life.

Yet, behind the scenes, there was a secret dance between the Madonna and the slut. Although one definition of slut is a woman who has many sexual partners, which I had, it is usually a term used for shaming. Consequently, when our kids lived at home, I would cover my sexy attire when we went out. My Madonna was telling me to be a good wife and mother. My mother's voice echoed, "Be a good girl and act like a lady." But my body would say, "Enjoy the pleasures of being the sexy slut."

Even when our sons grew into adulthood, we never told them that we had an open marriage and were Swingers. It just didn't sit well with me. I wanted to be their Madonna, always.

After our ayahuasca journey, Josh felt the need to be true to himself and our family by telling our sons. He wanted a guilt-free life but I just couldn't wrap my head around it. My boys were everything to me. I wanted them to look at me as their pure mother. Would they still look at me the same? Would they still respect and love me? I had my doubts, so Josh patiently waited for a shift.

Then our dear friend and editor put a note on one of our working copies of this book, "Your son was open and brave enough to tell you that he was gay. Don't you think he would be open and accepting of your Lifestyle?" I knew she was right.

As we continued writing, I knew things had to change. How could I share my story openly with strangers but keep it from my sons? My boys were adults (26 & 29) and I figured that they could handle the truth.

We invited our two sons and my son's husband over one Sunday afternoon. We sat in the living room and I took a deep breath. I opened my mouth to start but then said, "Your dad has something to tell you."

Josh's eyes darted my way. I had chickened out.

Josh told them that we were writing a book about our lives and our open relationship. A collective, "Phew" was felt in the room. They were relieved because they thought it must be something serious like a divorce or selling the house. We all laughed.

My Madonna and my Whore were finally united and my sons still love me.

Sharing our Secrets

We have a friend that says, "There are over 7.8 billion ways to lead a human life; I am only versed in one." Josh and I are only versed in two but because of the shared path, it has almost felt like one. The long-term relationship that we continue to create has been a dance of intimacy, at times doing our own dance moves yet sharing the same dance floor. Our choices have been our choices and they have worked for us. Your choices will be your choices and we hope that they lead to a life filled with pleasure, happiness and love.

With so many marriages ending with parting, we frequently get asked, "What is the secret to your happy marriage?" We don't have a single secret, but we have learned some things along the way...

Even at a young age while we were dating, I never felt jealous. Josh always had many girls as close friends. I always knew I had his heart. There was never a question of trust.

Josh and I chose to travel the path of openness. In our early years, before kids, there were intense periods of closeness which helped us establish a foundation for our new union. A budding relationship needs lots of time to fully take root. Once we became established, we turned our attention outward, toward the other parts of our lives that mattered: family, careers and friendships. But for our connection to last, we needed to return to the same attention, curiosity and nurturance of earlier times. Even mature trees need water and care if they are to survive.

Communication was key to nourishing our relationship. I learned to communicate by being honest and open with my feelings. I focused on the positive and avoided blame — nobody likes to feel that they aren't appreciated or seen by a partner. This created strength in our union. Sometimes when I just acknowledged that there was a distance between us, it had the effect of bringing us closer. We could set aside time to talk and come up with solutions to whatever was getting in the way of our connection. We developed empathy for each other, and a willingness to feel and understand the other person's point of view. This brought us even closer together.

As our open relationship grew, I liked to share my most intimate details with him. We created a safe space of non-judgment for each other. We found ways to appreciate and embrace the differences that set us apart and offered love and support no matter what. We encouraged each other to be exactly as we were and gave each other the opportunity to change over time. When we did change, we loved each other through all our transitions.

We expressed confidence in our abilities. We didn't have limitations to our dreams but instead allowed our imaginations to shape our ambitions in the most expansive way possible. This led to accomplishments that otherwise may have seemed far too ambitious. It also led to a life far grander than being married to the man I love and having a house with a color TV.

When I look back on my past, I do so without regrets and only see lessons that brought strength and wisdom. Even the times of extreme dieting and focusing on my appearance were merely stepping stones to who I am today. Seeing my own divinity, I've learned to recognize the divinity in all women. I look at my body as a temple and appreciate its feminine form and function no matter my age or stage of life. Rather than noticing a younger woman as competition, I notice the cycle of life reflected in her beauty. This reminds me to see my own radiance and shine with the attractiveness and strength of a diamond. This is the light that illuminates my world and fills me with contentment and joy.

In the last few years, my understanding of sex has shifted and my desires have taken a turn. Josh and I have gone from sport-fuckers to Demisexuals. Having a hook-up didn't appeal to us anymore and we really needed to know someone well before feeling a strong attraction. We craved more play friends with whom we could have an emo-

tional connection. We wanted something deeper and more fulfilling.
  We are creating just that. Now, physical appearance and gender
identity are not limiting factors. I want to experience sex as a meld-
ing of energies, not solely two bodies fucking. It is my birthright to
have pleasure with myself and whomever I choose. And lastly, we are
developing close friendships and expanding our strong community
of like-minded people.

The Fork in the Road

*Josh - It has taken me this long in the book to truly understand why I
chose to be in the Lifestyle. The revelation came one evening while we
were sitting in our hot tub (our Cauldron of Consciousness). Maggie was
sharing the realization behind her desire to have an open relationship.
It made total sense to both of us...she simply had a desire for more cock,
not just mine but a wide selection. An open relationship gave her the occasion to enjoy them. But it wasn't exactly the whole truth. The subse-
quent discovery of her trauma, and how it interplayed with her upbringing, helped her understand this hunger. She had experienced life-defining
events and it was her way of dealing with them. I respected that she
owned that. But what was it that enticed me? If it was cock for her, could
it be more pussy for me?*

*More pussy was too simple of an answer. It didn't resonate with me and
it wasn't a vision of myself that I recognized. There was an honesty to it
but it didn't reflect the whole truth. I really loved pussy but there must
have been some other catalyst. I have always loved women. I love everything about them, not just the sex parts.*

*At the time when we opened up our marriage, I didn't know Maggie's
driving force, nor did she. We both really embraced the whole Swinging
relationship model. It was obvious that she was having a great time, and
so was I. It was my role to do the research and plan our trips but she became the instigator of our sexcapades. It was exciting and fulfilling for
me to see her in a happy place. As I watched her exercise her power and
own her sexuality, it really turned me on. Big time.*

But that wasn't the whole story.

How I got into the Lifestyle required even more thought. I began to look back on many of the decisions that I had made since my youth. There appeared to be a consistent element. My life decisions were guided by how I embraced opportunity. I then had the sudden revelation that I was... duhn, duhn, duhn... an OPPORTUNIST.

Oh no, that didn't sound good.

Typically an opportunist is thought to be a person who exploits circumstances to create an advantage for themselves. An opportunist has little regard for principles, or what the consequences for others may be. That didn't seem to fit. I did care about the outcome for others and we chose our lovers accordingly. I was empathetic and compassionate yet if something or someone of interest was presented to me, I jumped on board. Our openness allowed me the freedom to do this.

After all of my self-reflection, the answers to why I co-created our open relationship became clear. They were many:

• Firstly, and most importantly, it really made me happy to see Maggie happy. There's an old adage that says, "Happy wife, happy life" and I can guarantee that my wife is happy, and that makes me...happy.

• I really did enjoy the pussy and loved having variety of sexual experiences, while maintaining the intimacy and security of a solid relationship with Maggie — the person I loved and admired.

• I craved the ego rush of being desired by someone else.

• I liked the social aspect of sharing common interests with our friends.

• The Lifestyle motivated me to look after my body and to keep in shape.

• I enjoyed watching Maggie use the Lifestyle to discover her power and self-acceptance.

• Mostly I love that it has strengthened our relationship. Yes, believe it or not, if done well, it can strengthen relationships.

Through our Lifestyle years, we played, learned, laughed and explored our sexuality together in our adult playground, not behind each other's backs but in front of each other's fronts. Choosing to do it that way was a huge turn on for both of us.

Since those days, I have come to understand that divine sexuality offers much more than all of the above. My interpretation of how our bodies work, how natural hormones reward me, and how sexual energy can be harvested, have guided me to my present reality. I am more mindful of our sexual practice and I embrace a more sacred approach to our sex life.

In addition to the happy juices, like dopamine, our practice has given me vitality and energy to expand me emotionally. Divine sex allows for a sacred intertwining of Qi/life force energy and has opened up an intimacy in my relationship(s) that I never knew existed. It allows us to uplift each other into a realm of bliss. I cannot think of another activity that is more enjoyable to practice regularly than sex.

I have a tattoo that features an image of a 'Y,' based on an old hobo icon that represents the fork in the road. This is a metaphor for my life's journey. I approach life's intersections as natural opportunities to change direction. This doesn't mean I'm just wandering or floundering; my clear desire has always been forward momentum and growth but I just didn't have a particular destination in mind. Perhaps I have a hobo spirit that clings to the freedom to choose which direction to go.

I will take you back to that first time Maggie fulfilled her fantasy with the black man in Hedo III. As I lay in that chaise lounge wondering if I was a loser, I could have continued to feed those thoughts. I could have thought, "My wife obviously doesn't love me. She wants other men..." I could have lost control of my thoughts and let them run amuck. Yet, I stopped myself in my tracks and decided to double back and take the other path. I tapped into the truth. I tapped into my love for myself and my love for my wife. I took the opportunity to mindfully forge the path that I wanted to create with Maggie. As Ralph Waldo Emerson once said, "Do not go where the path may lead, go instead where there is no path and leave a trail." This book is our trail for you, Dear Reader.

All of my choices have created the critical path that is my life. All of the stories included in this book are opportunities that I embraced. I always chose the one that was going to be the most enjoyable. Maggie and I have always been PSA — Pleasure Seeking Adults. We have leaned into pleasure. Pleasure is a practice and practice makes perfect.

So, What Does Enlightenment Mean?

Being enlightened doesn't mean that I sit on top of a mountain spewing words of deep wisdom. What it means to me is that I bring all the aspects of myself into the light, such as my insecurities, my shadows and my traumas. When I do this, they don't have the power to control or trigger me any longer. Since facing my sexual trauma, I now have more freedom of expression. This freedom doesn't just stay in the bedroom, it transfers to every area of my life. I don't need to lead with the warrior archetype because I know that the universe is conspiring for me, not against me. Even when something doesn't feel right, I sense it and have the voice to express it. I have the internal safety to be vulnerable, which allows for more fluidity.

The Oxford definition of vulnerable is "susceptible to physical or emotional attack or harm." I was susceptible in the past but I am not susceptible now. I am the keeper of my past stories but they are no longer the keeper of me.

I have learned that many of the behaviors that were adopted from society, parents and the church, were not important and I let go of those that weren't in my highest good. I was told by others what it meant to be me until I decided to sit in the driver's seat of my own life. Now *I* determine what it means to be me. When I allow myself to be me, I let go of my human identities such as mother, wife, designer, entrepreneur, and even writer. I don't turn to my ego for direction: I find answers through my heart-brain and my intuition.

Enlightenment is not a destination but continues to be a journey. I practice mind/body/spirit integration through Qi Gong, breath work, Kundalini Yoga and Neo-Tantra. With regular practice, I am able to vibrate at a high frequency and cast off anything that comes into my experience that isn't of the frequency of light and love. Thus, enlightenment is often a choice of which wolf I want to feed. The wolf of fear/gossip/anger etc. or the wolf of love.

I embody enlightenment every time I make choices that align with my values instead of those values that I was once taught. I now choose to make decisions that reflect my core values and unique ambitions. Even when others are advising me to take a path of societal success. I find true satisfaction in carving my own path. When I make the conscious effort to follow my heart rather than the dictates of social conformity, the path that I tread is uniquely my own.

Even though I have strong convictions about my life and how I should live it, I know that everyone else may not share the same belief system. I respect the beliefs of others and appreciate the diversity that exists in our world. I extend the courtesy of being open-minded to others and I appreciate the same in return. I have learned to accept the beauty in all of our differences. We are sacred mirrors for each other, each a unique expression of the Divine.

I have discovered that all of my growth has come from curiosity. I was curious about the Lifestyle and those years of participation allowed me to expand and experience pleasure in ways that I would not have otherwise. They say that "curiosity killed the cat" but my curiosity helped free me (and my pussy). Yet, I am never too old, too experienced or too wise to be curious. I am still reaching for a more profound stage of enlightenment by giving voice to the daily questions that form in my mind.

Josh and I have always moved towards experiences that felt light and pleasurable and away from experiences that felt dark and heavy. This is how we've navigated our open relationship for so many years. We have always been drawn to the light.

Josh - What does enlightenment mean to me? I should just cut and paste Maggie's previous response to this question, not in the spirit of copying but because our journey together has (almost always) been a co-creation. I will add this though...both Maggie and I travel lightly. What does that look like? We've reached the point in our lives where we've let go of all the old stories that were weighing us down. In addition, we've let go of all worry of what will happen in the future. This allows all of our energy to be in the present moment. With all of our energy in the present, we wield the full power of creation. We call it the "Now" moment.

So, where has this journey brought Maggie and me? Knowing that one way to measure the efficacy of anything is by the results, the results are as follows:

Physically — we have more energy than we have been for years. It has helped to heal and balance our bodies. We honor ourselves daily with exercise and healthy eating habits. We have lowered the pace of our everyday lives. Our sex doesn't get old, stale or repetitive. We don't need lust to enjoy sexual energy. We like to hang out and play with others that are a decade younger than us, and they seem to enjoy us. It is so exciting and fulfilling when we can celebrate our bodies and sexuality together. We have become filled with abundant vitality.

It has changed us emotionally — we are more empathetic, more positive, happy and satisfied. It helped us to open up and we have become more joyful and playful. Our communication is better than ever before. There is more order, balance and harmony in our lives.

It has changed us mentally —we are more grounded and centered. Our minds and intellect have become sharper. We are more intuitive and more positive. We have fully embraced being the conscious creators of our lives.

It has changed us spiritually — we feel united with our partners' spirits. We mutually transform and uplift each other into a realm of bliss and wholeness. We feel the connection in our hearts and that part of ourselves outside our physical body...dare we say, our souls?

And lastly, Maggie and I have become spiritually enlightened. We live from the Everlasting Present Moment with an awareness of all that surrounds us. We are content.

We can honestly say, "Been there, done that, and glad we did." Our Lifestyle sexploits broadened our awareness of all sexual activities with ourselves and others. It exposed us to many different cultures and perspectives. The mandatory good communication has provided us with a much greater understanding of ourselves and each other. It has helped us discover our own Divine sexuality.

From Zen Den to Church of Unreasonable Happiness

As mentioned, Josh and I met at the tender ages of 7 and 8 in Sunday school. One of the main purposes of attending church was to commune with like-minded people gathered to worship God. Our Christian upbringing came with a foundation of ethics that instilled morals and values. Yet, despite Josh and my differing gender experiences, neither of us understood the idea that something as enjoyable as sex could be a sin.

What we did take into our adulthood was the teaching, "Love thy neighbor as thyself," along with, "Do unto others as you would have others do unto you." These became the foundation of our morality.

After our journeys with ayahuasca, where we found ourselves void of ego at one with the All, our understanding of these precepts deepened. We realized that everything is so intrinsically connected that when we do something to our neighbor, we are also doing it to ourselves. The Golden Rule is a universal law.

When we created our "Zen Den" room, our sole purpose was to make the space a safe environment for meditation, journaling, yoga, and playing. Our *soul* purpose was to design a place where we could invite others to gather and feel love and compassion for each other. For our happily consenting guests, we would be open and vulnerable to share ourselves in whichever way we desired.

A friend of ours who was caught up in the atmosphere one night suggested we call our space "The Church Of Unreasonable Happiness." We loved the idea.

Our "church" is a place where we remove sin from consensual sexual pleasure. We believe that we are all gods and goddesses, here to create our own heavens on Earth. We honor the temples of our bodies. We gather to show each other tenderness, kindness, and joy. Our Golden Rule is LOVE.

What if your *sole* purpose is to be happy? What would *your* life look like then?

When we touch
the place in our lives
where sexuality and
spirituality come together,
we touch our wholeness
and the fullness of our power,
and at the same time
our connection with a
power larger than
ourselves.

- Author: Judith Plaskow

F*cking Our Way to Enlightenment

"Josh & Maggie's" first couples profile picture

The early years

Hedonism III photo op!

Paris is for lovers

Glamming it up for Hollywood

This naughty angel is in command
Radiant at Rythmia, Costa Rica

Not your standard boat cruise attire

One night in Monaco

Traveling the world

The Playrooms are ready

Working with the LLV crew

What do *you* wear when shopping?

Destinations near and far

An evening in the Belvedere castle

Cruising on the Adriatic

What do *you* wear when...

Burning man
Bikes and
Boobies

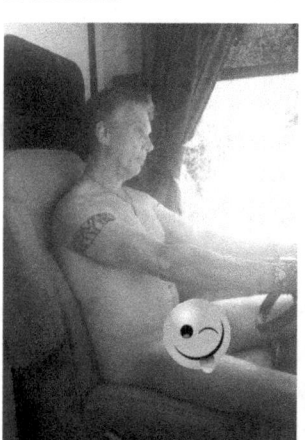

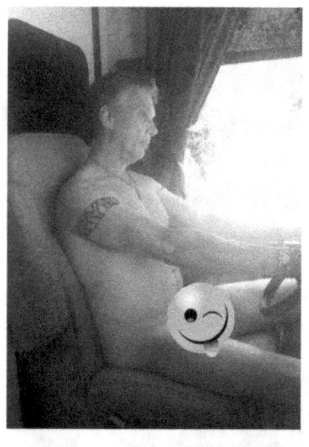

A few Lifestyle website profile images

F*cking Our Way to Enlightenment

So, Why are you Here?

Since you are here reading this book, you are likely open to discovering new or alternate forms of relationships for yourself or with your partner. Or maybe you are just curious about how sex and energy can intertwine. Either way, you have now been exposed to our story. You may not agree with our life choices or fully understand our ramblings but your curiosity has been a step in your personal exploration.

You *Can* Have Your Cake and Eat it Too!

When opening your relationship, the Lifestyle may be the perfect place to experiment. It is also a great way to expand your sex life when single. A big part of joining the Lifestyle community is finding ways to meet new people with similar interests, but you need to know yourself and what you are looking for first.

Intimate play provides an opportunity to learn about the sexual styles of others. When you experience those styles, you may learn more about yourself and what you like.

Some look at Swinging, polyamorous or open relationships as a band-aid for their partnership. Through our observation, that doesn't seem to work. We can't think of anyone we have met over the years that have successfully revived a dead marriage by having sex with others. We have a friend, Fleur, who says that polyamory and the Swinger Lifestyle are triple black diamond runs. You don't want to be attempting them before you have the skills, otherwise you will end up hurting yourself and others. These skills include excellent communication, honesty, non-reactivity, and the ability to prioritize your primary relationship(s). When you hit the black diamonds, they should be exhilarating not filled with pain and suffering.

On the other hand, playing can satisfy the burning sexual desire of being with others. The Lifestyle allowed Josh and I to have our indulgences with the blessing of our spouse while still honoring our marriage. We play well with each other and we play well with others.

Sometimes the issues in a relationship may be different appetites for sex. Sex drive can be influenced by many things including stress, family life, early trauma, age-related conditions, etc. Not every couple has evenly matched mojos. We see that a lot in relationships where the man is significantly older. It is getting quite common to find Hot Wife situations where the female has younger partners or a Bull (stud, typically single) to service her. She gets her satisfaction, he gets a happy wife, and they get something really hot to talk about.

It is up to you and your partner to decide on your relationship agreements. For many couples, it isn't considered cheating if their partner is with a same-sex playmate. If one (or both of you) is bisexual, then playing is the only way that you can be fully sexually satisfied. We feel it's unfair to limit a bisexual person's sexual expression to only one gender. Bottom line, whatever your sexual preferences, it's up to you and your partner to negotiate what works for both of you.

It is difficult to find a relationship that fulfills all of your romantic or sexual needs. Some couples are lucky, but many feel trapped in a sexually stagnant marriage. If this sounds familiar, it is important that you communicate with your partner. You may want to find a counsellor who specializes in non-monogamy that will help you express your desires and find a way for you to get them satisfied within your relationship. It might not be easy at first. Many of us are not interested in normative monogamy but for most people, it is the only approach to which we've been conditioned.

Playing with others provides an opportunity to have all your sexual needs met by a variety of people in many different ways. The relationship cycle shows us that in most couples, the flame of passion dims through time. You're still best friends with a deep emotional connection but you don't jive in the bedroom. You don't want to break up, so you find play partners. It is best when the play partners are found in a way that honors your relationship because "cheating" (or non-consensual non-monogamy) is betrayal and can lead to the breakdown of the relationship. Why do this when there is another way?

The best way to avoid damaging your relationship is to be honest and open about your boundaries, your fears, and your desires. Success comes from trust and communication and not taking shortcuts. Make your relationship a safe vessel for sharing. The last thing you want is for your relationship to suffer instead of flourish.

The most common response that we get when we tell people that we are in an open relationship is, "I could never do that. I'm too jealous." If non-monogamy is something that interests you, you have to do the personal work to change your jealousy into something else. It becomes easy when you have the ability to perceive your partner's play partners as friends, not competition. To do this, you have to be secure in yourself and secure in your connection with your partner. Being secure in yourself is an inside job but when you do the work, playing with others becomes fun.

It is interesting to note that some people who have been around the Lifestyle for years never take the step of actually having sex with other people. Soft Swing is an excellent way of reducing some of the anxieties that go along with Full Swap. Some people don't even go as far as Soft Swing, but enjoy participating in the Lifestyle just for the fun friendships. They may get their thrill from attending sexy parties where they can let loose and not feel judged. Some are nudists and appreciate an environment where people can safely show a bit of skin and get their own personal freak on. The nudity, flirting and foreplay is enough for them.

We have created a questionnaire at the back of this book to help you discover the play styles that turn both you and your partner on. It is a good thing to revisit it after six months and see if there are any changes that you may have experienced. We have also included a lexicon (an 'Alt-Dic' - alternate dictionary) to help you discover unfamiliar terms.

If you plan to participate in the Lifestyle, there are many terms that you will need to familiarize yourself with, things like: Play, Play Friends, Unicorns, Hot Wife, Vanilla, Hall Pass, Full Swap, Soft Swap, etc. By studying the Alt Dic in the back of the book, you'll familiarize yourselves with these terms.

Pleasure Seeking Adults

As mentioned, Lifestyle clubs weren't around in our town when Josh and I first started Swinging so our early years were mostly filled with house parties and travel. We had a pretty good tribe back then and we still see some of these couples twenty years later. There are more of us out there than you think.

I remember a certain degree of awkwardness back then. We were all exploring and pretty new at opening our marriage. We were discovering our boundaries and fears while balancing them with exploring our desires. There weren't any guidebooks to help us navigate. We were exploring new territory and discovering the best ways to keep our relationship healthy and a priority. We were leaving the old paradigm of marriage that was handed down to us through our parents and society to craft the marriage that suited us.

There is a saying, "You don't know what you don't know." When you first start exploring opening a relationship, it is the time when you will discover your partner's desires and boundaries and see how they align with your own. It can be an anxious time for some so make sure you keep your communication clear and your heart open to change. Remember Josh's honesty when he didn't meet my new play partner before I went off to play? He felt confident enough to speak up and say that my choice didn't work for him. This clear communication has been key to our thriving in our open relationship. Bottling up feelings is not being open with yourself nor with your partner.

Telling others that you are now in the Lifestyle can elicit a wide assortment of reactions, some of them surprising. The feeling of judgment can be a strong weapon against your personal choices, especially when they come from some of your closest friends. Just remember, no rule says you need to tell anyone. Period. Openness and Honesty with your partner doesn't have to translate to your whole social circle.

Fortunately, Josh and I were both in an industry that was accepting of alternative ways of living. We didn't have a wild life of fucking strangers every weekend. We raised children and had to balance our needs with theirs. Locally, our Lifestyle events didn't happen that often, but when they did, they allowed us to be true to ourselves and our desires. That was liberating. At the same time, we were also very careful about whom we let into our secret kink. There is a fine line between putting yourselves out there to attract like-minded people and keeping enough of it covered so that the morality police don't come down on you.

Remember that you will be judged, not by some higher being, but by some of your closest friends. Stay true to yourself and your feelings. The right people will begin to form around you. They will be your tribe, even if it's only during your vacations.

So, how do you find playmates or at least like-minded people with all this secrecy? One way is by dropping little clues in conversation, like "adult resort" or "play time" and assessing the response. It will get easier with your experience.

There was a time not long ago when you needed to find play partners on Craigslist or classified newspaper ads. The Internet has made all of this much easier. Currently, many Swinger/Lifestyle sites are catering to all sorts of people and sexual desires but some are better than others. It is worth the energy to explore a few local sites to see if you click with the type of members on the site.

Once you decide to put yourself out there, you will want to create a "handle" or name to call your new online identity. We have met couples that use "Swinger names" (think "pen name" but more like "fuck name") as an additional layer of privacy. Not everyone has a career or family life that could withstand a possible "outing."

The next step is taking some photos. Just like any dating site, how you present yourself will determine the response you receive. "A picture is worth a thousand words" and it is definitely what attracts potential playmates. If you are married, make sure to include photos of both of you.

Typical Lifestyle sites will have questionnaires that require you to describe yourself and your preferences when setting up your profile. These will help open up the communications or expectations with your partner. Use our questionnaire to familiarize yourselves with the terms as well as your boundaries and desires. We've met hundreds of couples during our adventures and every one of them approaches it differently.

In addition to the Internet, local Lifestyle clubs are fun to attend and make some new friends. Also, adult XXX stores can be a good source of what is going on in your community. They may have a notice board or the staff may help direct you.

Alternatively, you may decide, like us, that a vacation away from home is the best way to explore the Lifestyle. Travel destinations, cruise ships, and hotel takeovers are a great way to expand your play friend zone. These may be the ideal container, away from your everyday life, to probe your desires. The week or two you spend together is a great way to get to know play partners. Getting away from your familiar territory may just help you to relax and loosen some of your inhibitions. If so, we've included some great options in the Resource section at the back of the book.

Protocols in the Lifestyle community favor women making the decisions on playtime with whom, when and where. This has been a good guideline for us. Josh's penis brain would have made different decisions than my heart brain; no sex is better than regrettable sex. We have witnessed women who have been coerced into the Lifestyle by a dominant partner. Once the party starts, it usually becomes clear who is actually in charge. We circumvent those domineering men who aim to control their wives. Even if this is their kink, it's not something we tend to relate well to. We have seen couples that the male half is always in command, directing their partner. She may go along with his request to satisfy his desire. The woman's feelings are compromised and undesirable emotional states become evident.

Frequently, these relationships break down because of inequities.

Even with the females taking the lead, the situation isn't perfect. Equally, the female partner may try to dominate the relationship if she doesn't take her spouse's preferences, boundaries, fears and desires into consideration. Remember to respect your partner's wishes. Even if you're steering the ship, not everyone is ready to jump in at your request.

Love and sex in the Lifestyle can be confusing, especially in the formative years of an open relationship. A physical connection doesn't have to be confused with an emotional one. If it does, you need to ask yourself, what am I looking for? Is it ground-and-pound animalistic sex or is it a more psychological one? Either is fine as long as everyone involved is on the same page.

What do you want to get out of it? Is it simply a physical fulfillment or are you looking for an emotional security blanket? Are you doing this for yourself or for your life partner? Are you acting of your own free will?

An intimate encounter will bring up all sorts of feelings that you may not be ready for. We notice that many Newbies can sometimes form a fatal attraction to their first playmates. There is something in our DNA that tells us if we lick it, then it's ours. Or, like me, you feel some obligation to hang around and be close as some kind of gesture to them. You don't want them to think you used them just for your gratification. Guilt can be a powerful motivator for our actions.

I had a monogamous friend ask a question. "Do you ever have emotional feelings with your other play partners?" My response was: "Oh no, I just fuck them. Josh is my beloved one." Sex doesn't have to have an emotional attachment to be good. But you do need to have some attachment for it to be amazing. It is a fine balance.

Healthy relationships require C.A.R.E.

We were recently asked by a friend who is a couples counsellor, "What are the most important points of a healthy relationship?" After considering his query, we came up with the four corner posts that we call CARE:

C - Communication. Without the ability to express ourselves and listen to each other, partners cannot connect deeply. We are all busy in our lives, but not communicating with your partner is a shortcut that will damage your relationship. It doesn't matter how well you know and love each other, you can't read your partner's mind. When you respect your partner, you will want to hear what they are saying. Communication includes body language, tone of voice, and facial expressions. All of these convey a message. Good communication also involves being quiet and deeply listening, not just waiting for the chance to give your response.

A - Appreciation. We all crave positive attention. Appreciating your partner by expressing gratitude or acknowledging his/her actions reinforces your love. It lets your partner know that you are aware of the gifts that he/she brings to your life.

R - Respect. This recognizes the unalienable right of human beings to have free will and agency in their lives. It also represents itself in your admiration for him/her as a person.

E - Eros. The passion and love that you have for each other. It's that fiery sexual energy that keeps you thriving.

We have identified a few additional key qualities that we have seen in successful relationships. These are all elements that we have incorporated into our union:

1) Validation. Having your partner listen and understand what you are saying is paramount to a solid connection. It is important to show your interest and be engaged in his/her thoughts. It's typical to disagree on many topics, as long as you can respect where each other is coming from because he/she is coming from a lived experience that is different than yours. Recognizing that someone's feelings and thoughts make sense can show that we are listening nonjudgmentally and can help build a stronger relationship with your partner.

2) Curiosity. Ask questions about each other. What are his/her feelings, and needs? Make the questions thought-provoking to encourage a deeper response.

3) Play to each other's strengths. Few situations are 50/50 in terms of day-to-day life. Depending on the task, one partner may need to put in more effort. This is good as long as it isn't the same partner doing

all the giving. Know when to use your strengths and give your partner the opportunity to do the same.

4) Being right isn't always right. The American author and psychiatrist, Gerald Jampolsky, wrote, "You can be right or you can be happy." The compulsive need to be right can be incredibly destructive in a relationship. When couples respect each other, they can accept not being right in favor of maintaining the spirit of teamwork. The desire to be right (or to have superiority over another) is highly competitive. Who wants to do that when you're part of a team? There is no "I" in team.

5) Don't be afraid of honesty. The truth can be uncomfortable, but a couple that has mutual respect isn't afraid to express themselves. They can deal with the feelings of anger that might come from discussing harsh truths because they have the bigger picture in mind.

6) Do little things for each other. Love is a verb. It isn't just about expressing the three magic words, it's the actions that give living proof of the words. For loving couples, these gestures are second-nature: a simple love note, a slightly longer and sensual kiss goodbye, or making your partner tea/coffee first thing in the morning can make your partner feel special. Surprise your spouse as you did when you were first dating. Healthy relationships aren't just about trying in the beginning; they are about expressing love in the present moment, and stringing those moments together to create a lifetime of love.

7) Know how to give one another space (this is a big part of respect for us). As much as it is important to be supportive and engaged, allow your spouse to solve his/her own problems. Trying to solve all problems solves nothing and undermines your spouse's belief in his/her own resources. When you truly know each other's strengths and weaknesses you will know when to step back. Let go of the control and let your spouse figure it out on his/her own. Have faith.

8) Take care of yourself. It isn't enough to take care of your partner, you also need to take care of yourself. You can't have a solid relationship if you don't have a solid relationship with yourself. Investing in yourself will show your partner that you want to be your best self. Eating healthy, exercising, getting enough sleep and drinking

lots of water are examples of self-care.

9) Be a good role model. When couples have mutual respect, they set good examples for their kids. They don't argue in front of them or speak negatively about the other person to the children, or others. Healthy couples also make time for date nights and time together.

You are your children's first loves so modelling loving behavior is key.

The Big Question...

How do you tell your partner you want to have sex with someone else? We suggest that you don't, unless you already have an amazing relationship that you want to improve by adding novelty. If you don't have a great connection, work on your connection first.

We cannot stress this enough...create the dream relationship with your partner. Without this connection, this Lifestyle could be destructive. Without this connection, inviting others into your relationship will put a spotlight on all the things that aren't working. Without this connection, you won't be fun to play with as marital tensions will be felt by others. However, when a solid relationship is created, the Lifestyle becomes additive not subtractive. We have always made time for each other before and after playtime to confirm our commitment to each other. If you are distracted and don't emphasize the importance of your relationship or if your partner is unattentive, the last thing that you want is to invite more people into your relationship.

Gary Chapman's book, *The Five Love Languages - How to Express Heartfelt Commitment to your Mate,* may give you some tools to strengthen your connection with your partner. Understanding the love languages and how they impact your relationship is a great way to understand your partner's (and your own) preferences and outlook on romance, love, and sexuality. Each of us gives and receives love in preferred ways. These ways are:

1. Physical touch - eg. A back rub
2. Quality time - eg. Thirty minutes of undivided attention

3. Acts of service - eg. Cleaning the kitchen, taking out the trash
4. Receiving gifts - eg. A thoughtful gift showing that your partner is truly seen
5. Words of affirmation - eg. Telling them what you love about them

We also include being "present" with your partner by minimizing any distractions including cell phones, television, etc.

Once you have established an amazing connection with your partner, it is time to have a discussion. You both need to feel safe, connected and confident in your relationship. Here are some ideas to help get the conversation started.

• Get him/her to read this book and have an open discussion about it.

• Suggest a movie or a TV show that features Swinging or open relationships as a theme, then talk about it. Allow your imagination to expand your desires by completing the sentence, "What if we..." Then talk about it. See what emotions surface.

• If you like porn, watch movies featuring multiple partners. Again, see what excites both of you.

• Visit a few Lifestyle websites, and read blogs or articles. Allow yourselves time to digest the concept of "what if we...." Play it out in your minds and see what emotions it stirs up. Does it bring up jealousy? Compersion? Excitement?

• Propose visiting a Swingers' club.

• Some cities that enjoy an active Lifestyle community have "Meet and Greet" functions. They are a great way to get out and experience the atmosphere and meet some of the people in your area. Your local online Swinger site or sex shop are good places to check for any of these events. They can be enjoyed without the added pressure of being on a date with another couple or single.

• *Always* be supportive of your partner's feelings and desires. Your suggestion to Swing can be interpreted in many different ways. Without a proper understanding of what Swinging entails, the idea can be taken poorly.

• The wrong question to ask is: How can I convince my partner to get into Swinging? *This is not a forced activity.* It should be fun and mutual and a decision that makes you both comfortable and excited.

When you do decide to make the request, there is no guaranteed approach so tread carefully. Your partner's response will depend on many things including: how it's presented, the health status of your relationship, your cultural/religious background, and his/her open-mindedness.

It doesn't matter which side of this conversation you are on. What does matter is that you hold space for your partner, without judgment.

It is easy for you to feel inadequate with the thought of a partner wanting to sexplore someone other than you. Feel free to express how you are feeling, even if it makes you feel vulnerable. Watch your body language, facial expressions, and tone of voice, even if the topic doesn't sit well with you. Any perceptions of your disapproval or rejection of the topic could lead to unpleasant emotions and conflict or cause your lover to shut down.

It may not be an easy task for you to reveal your deepest, darkest fantasies. But to be truly understood, you need to be able to communicate freely and safely without judgment. Watch your timing. If you plan to bring up the idea of having sex with someone else, find a time with little or no distractions and when you are both connecting emotionally and sexually. Or book a session with a counsellor who is versed in non-monogamy. They may help you get the support you need to navigate your relationship into new territory.

No matter what your partner's response is, it's important to always ask them to express their boundaries, fears and desires at the forefront and to understand that this is his/her perspective.

Josh - For years, we had a friend who would have the same conversation with us about opening his marriage. It always went like this:
Steve: I think I want to explore the Lifestyle with my wife.
Josh: Then do.
Steve: But I don't know if it would work for me.
Josh: Then don't.
Now, repeat that conversation a few times and you will see how difficult it is for some people to allow themselves the freedom to explore. Our friend Steve and his wife never did participate in the Lifestyle.

We've found that many friends and acquaintances are interested but when it's time to dive in, their insecurities hold them back. We believe the baggage of social norms plays a role as well. Alternative Lifestyles aren't always looked upon fondly and some people just don't want to be judged by their peers or anyone else for that matter.

Communication is Key

Do you really know what your partner likes? Or dislikes? Do you know what turns him/her on? To share sexual fantasies, there has to be an environment of trust and nonjudgment. If you can't tell your partner that you like pistachio ice cream over chocolate without feeling judged, chances are you won't be able to share your deepest desires. Work on establishing a safe environment first.

Take our sexual preference questionnaire at the back of the book. It will help guide the conversation with your partner about your personal likes/dislikes/fantasies. And most important, talk honestly, openly, and frequently.

Josh - We experienced an awkward situation once with a newly married couple that was also new to the Lifestyle. The husband had organized a party but had not consulted his wife about it. Everyone could feel the tension between them and it made the mood uncomfortable. It put the brakes on the evening and messed up what could have been a fun party. We chose not to get involved and gently removed ourselves from the situation.

Sexual Desire Discrepancy (SDD)

In simple terms, Sexual Desire Discrepancy is when two partners do not share the same levels of sex drive or libido (Mark & Murray, 2012). In addition, they may not share the same desires, interests, or kinks.

Sexual compatibility is a fluid concept. People are constantly changing, and with them, so are their libido levels and desires. Certain life events, hormone changes, or behavioural changes can cause shifts in a couple's sexual compatibility. Physical limitations may be present, including pain or erectile dysfunction issues. It can cause significant distress in a relationship if you have different needs. This can reveal itself in the Lifestyle as a difference in the desire to play with others.

If someone doesn't feel attractive or is self-conscious, it may be hard for him/her to relax into the arms of a new acquaintance or be physically exposed to strangers. Be patient with each other. Be vulnerable enough to talk about what is holding you back. These are important areas to discuss if you are interested in opening up your relationship. And don't be discouraged if you are experiencing SDD with your partner. Sexual Desire Discrepancy is one of the most commonly reported reasons for couples to seek therapy (Ellison, 2002).

Whichever direction you choose to go in your relationship, it needs to be 100% in agreement with your partner. Without that, you are practicing non-consensual non-monogamy. This book is about consensual non-monogamy. There is no reason for you to cheat your partner out of the truth. Be bold enough to stand in the truth.

More on Jealousy

Almost everyone experiences jealousy to some degree, and Swingers are no exception. The fantasy of watching your partner with another person might be a turn-on, but the reality can be much different. If you're jealous, you may fear losing your position to someone else. You can find yourself feeling left out, intimidated, and insecure. These feelings may also change from experience to experience and playmate to playmate.

When you've realized that you are dealing with some jealousy issues around Swinging, the first step is to speak with your partner. Sharing your concerns with him/her may be enough to make you feel secure. It can be an excellent opportunity to talk about your feelings. Identify what is causing these feelings. There is always a reason to feel jealous and once you find the root cause it becomes easier to find ways to overcome it.

Having relationship rules can also bring a sense of comfort. Just hearing from your partner that your relationship is a priority and that Swinging is just sex could be enough to keep emotions in check – particularly if you have these conversations regularly. Open communication is a great preventative measure to keep jealousy away.

If these things haven't worked and you are still feeling jealous, it might be time to visit a professional. Look for therapists in your area, and see if anyone specializes in non-monogamous relationships. This might help you work through the problems you are experiencing in an open relationship.

You may have to accept that having an open relationship isn't the right thing for you at any particular time. There are many reasons why it might be time for you to stop Swinging. Having a baby is a good example of this. It is something that you can come back to in the future. It may be time to work on yourself and your relationship. Once you have had your reset and feel more secure, you can return to Swinging and try it again with a fresh start.

Another hurdle that open couples can encounter is *envy*. It is a truth in the Lifestyle that the dating scene is not an equal opportunity activity. We have seen and heard that women receive a much greater response than men. When one person is getting all the attention, it can put pressure on a relationship. It is also easy to be envious when watching another couple that is highly successful and popular. Instead of having animosity towards them, observe their behaviour and style. Look to see what it is that makes them stand out above the others. Take note and see if there is something that you can do in your way to make yourself attractive to others. An example is being good at oral sex and being the guy who satisfies all the woman.

The Bottom Line

Are you in or are you out? It is that simple sometimes. If it works for you… great! If it doesn't, stop, that's ok too. At least you will know the answer and never suffer from the "what if's?"

It still strikes me as strange that anyone could have any moral objection to someone else's sexuality. It's like telling someone else how to clean their house.

— River Phoenix

Why Are You Here?

Josh and Maggie's Lifestyle Insights, Observations and Opinions

Fifty ways to Keep Your Lover(s)

For those of you who have read the book, *F*cking Our Way to Enlightenment,* you already know that Josh and I have enjoyed over forty years of marriage with over twenty years in an open relationship. This guide is the juicy insider secrets that you were promised. Based on our experiences, we offer you practices that can help you navigate your own interpretation of non-monogamy.

Although our personal journey started with the Swinger Lifestyle and has morphed into something different, this guide will focus mainly on Swinging. The Lifestyle may be a good place to begin your exploration as the rules of engagement are fairly standardized. In addition, there is an emphasis on keeping the primary relationship as the central focus. Thus, this framework is like non-monogamy with training wheels.

The following advice and recommendations are based on our actual experiences in the Swinging Lifestyle community. Your experiences will differ from ours. This is a very personal journey and what works for us may not work for you. These points are merely our observations, from our points of view and may be used to develop the best practices to keep your relationship sacrosanct.

Let's start with an easy one...

1) Get your priorities straight

Know your personal priorities...your spouse and family are first, then everything else follows including the "sextra-curricular" activities. If you keep these straight in your mind, your heart, and with your actions, the rest will be easy.

How do Josh and I ensure that others aren't a distraction or don't take away from our connection? By making our connection the priority. We take time during the week to turn off all devices and connect with each other. Then when we open up to play with others, they have an additive effect, not a subtractive one.

2) Know your relationship preference

The terms "open relationship" or "consensual non-monogamy," are terms for all relationship styles that are open, honest and consensual forms of non-monogamy.

Some people think of an open relationship as an emotionally monogamous/sexually promiscuous one, but this is just one type of open relationship.

We are aware of 3 main types of non-monogamy. There are a number of sub-types to these examples but these are the most common:

I) **Swinger** - this is where the couple is primary. They are bonded together and really know how to communicate. They have a sense of community and attend organized events such as cruises, hotel takeovers, house parties, etc. They play mostly together.

II) **Open relationship/marriage** - They like to play together or separately. They have full trust in their primary partner. Usually, they look for a temporary hookup but often have regular play partners. They may or may not talk about their playtime with their primary partner. Also referred to as "monogamish."

III) **Polyamory** - They may not have a primary partner. They could be in a throuple or quad relationship or more. They are romantically involved with all their partners. The participants are all emotionally love-bonded.

3) Establish relationship agreements

Establishing ground rules starts with good communication. Make sure you are both on the same page. It is important to start this journey on a good foundation of honesty to support your life together. Here are some points to consider:

• Begin by sharing what you are looking for in an open relationship.

• Create a list of your personal desires and boundaries: the things that interest you, and the things that are hard "no's."

• Discuss the reasons behind each item on your list and ensure that you understand each other's motivations. Let love lead.

• Agree on your personal limitations around your future playtime.

• Discuss what would happen if one of you chooses to no longer participate.

• Consider how being in the Lifestyle could affect your career or family dynamics if people found out.

• Keep talking and communicating openly. This is not the time to be shy or succumb to any choices that do not work for you.

You can expect this list to evolve with your experience and growth. You can also expect to make mistakes. You can make all sorts of agreements but eros/passion, can cloud the decision-making process.

Take time to discuss the topics in our sexual preference questionnaire. It might introduce you to play styles that you are currently not aware of but may come up in future encounters. It is important that you and your partner understand each other's expectations and desires before you play with others.

4) Consider which types of play excite you

Another topic for discussion is what types of play you are interested in exploring. Some couples have hard limits that restrict things like kissing on the lips, their favorite sexual position, or anything anal. These agreements can help ensure that play stays playful and doesn't exceed personal comfort levels.

In the Lifestyle community, there are different types of play. The most recognized of these are:

Voyeur - They will be the couple at the back of the room, or off to the side checking out the action. This is a real turn-on for many couples, especially Newbies just starting to dip their toes into the scene. It can be a good way for couples to express their attractions and the kind of play that excites them in a safe and non-threatening manner. This can also help by ironing out the jitters and expressing fears when others aren't involved. Think of it as the bunny hills of Swinging.

Soft Swing - This refers to everything from sex with just your partner in front of another couple, to everything except penetration. Every couple has their boundaries and these should be discussed ahead of time.

Girl/Girl - This is prevalent in the Lifestyle. A woman's touch, skin, lips, and energy is a welcome addition to many females. It doesn't always need to be about penetration. The girl/girl action can include everything from passionate kissing to "grab the strap-on" and giddy up!

Guy/Guy - As discussed, despite the openness of Swingers in general, there is still a stigma about male-to-male contact. It appears that the new generation of Swingers is more open to it than the old guard (but it could just be the friends we keep). We find it strange that so many men have this fear of "crossing swords" in the bedroom except when there are 2 cocks all wrapped up in one hot, wet pussy. This is where open and honest communication is important so that no one gets offended.

Full Swing/with limitations - We have seen so many variations of this. It is your choice if you want or need to put limitations on your sexual practices. You should not feel pressured to do anything you're not comfortable with, ever. These can include:

• Kissing for some couples is too intimate. Kissing is a part of our experience and brings an intimacy that we enjoy sharing with others. That choice isn't for everyone nor should you expect it to be.

• Anal is another biggie. Many couples feel this is one area reserved for the primary partner and keep it special between themselves. Others simply don't like butt stuff.

• Same-room play is also a popular choice. We love to see each other being pleasured. Establish your rules before heading to the bedroom. This will make everyone more comfortable.

Josh - We experienced an extreme example of "full swing with no limitations" at a resort in Mexico. One couple had brought a portable sex swing and had set it up in their room. It was the woman's birthday and she wanted to have fun all day long. So to fulfill her wish, her husband invited random guys to stop by in the afternoon to fuck his wife while she reclined in the swing. They left the door open to their room and the guys lined up outside just to take their turn. She seemed to love it and the husband seemed to enjoy the procession of men. They both had a memorable day. If gang bangs are your thing, a Lifestyle event is one of the best places to find experienced men or women to fulfill your fantasy.

5) Be comfortable with your sexual orientation

One of the larger Swinger blog sites recently sent out a State of Play Swinger Survey. The data below comes from responses from 1,018 people about their Lifestyle preferences & activity. The results of that survey reflect our experience.

It was interesting to see significant differences between men & women (19.9% of men selected "bisexual" compared to 58.4% of women) as well as between younger & older Swingers (43.3% of Swingers under 40 selected "bisexual" compared to 20.7% of swingers who are 50 & up). Based on several comments received (and our observations in the Lifestyle through the years), it appears that men and older Swingers tend to feel less comfortable exploring options outside of a heteronormative mindset. We expect to see some shifts over time as the broader society moves towards a more inclusive, welcoming stance. (This information was summarized from swingershelp.com.)

Josh - My experience has found that the majority of men enjoy watching girl/girl play and we often find them encouraging their partners to engage in it. It has also revealed that there is a general avoidance of any guy/guy contact. There is a surprising level of homophobia by men in the Lifestyle has always seemed a bit hypocritical to me. Just go to any Swinger site and look at the profiles. Most women list their preference as either bi or bi-comfortable. Rarely do you find men stating the same, although the trend does appear to be slowly evolving with the newer generations. Whatever your personal choices are, it is important to make your intentions or desires clear with your partners just in case they aren't on the same page as you.

6) Cultivate compersion

The word compersion is loosely defined as the opposite of jealousy. This is when you are feeling joy or happiness (and sometimes arousal) for your partner when they are experiencing pleasure with a person other than you.

Our society has made monogamy a practice and our evolution has trained us to protect our mating relationships. Compersion requires us to go against our biology and reach for something outside the norm. It doesn't always come naturally to people.

The term was originally coined in the late 80s by the Keristan Commune, a polyamory community in San Francisco. The roots of the concept are much older than that and require us to access parts of the self that are outside of our ego and the conditioned "fight or flight" response.

You are in the land of compersion when:

• You experience a real turn-on when you see your spouse/partner with another person (although this could also be a cuckold fetish that may or may not include jealousy).
• He/she is fucking them hard and they are liking it.
• You and your spouse/partner lock eyes together and feel each other's acceptance just knowing that you are extremely happy and pleasured at the moment.
• You can feel the love and the energy flowing between you.
• You know that your connection with your partner is unwavering.

But what about jealousy? It is a very natural emotion and sometimes the emotional alarm is going off because something is actually wrong. Your partner isn't giving you the attention or affection you need, or maybe they betrayed a promise or agreement you have between you. This of course makes you feel unstable or upset. You may have some insecurities that you need to discuss with your partner. Sometimes we get worried about him/her having a conversation with an attractive stranger. You are concerned that your spouse may be more interested in him/her than you.

As described earlier, communication is key here. Expressing your discomfort will reveal what the issues are and allow you to address them. Jealousy is part of the human emotional spectrum, and there is no way to avoid it entirely. Non-monogamous people tend to just spend more time processing their feelings of jealousy and have more practice in dealing with it. With enough practice, good communication, and by following partnership rules/boundaries, jealousy may stop being so big and overwhelming. And with time, compersion can appear in its place.

Start with empathy and understanding your partner's emotions. If you aren't great at reading someone's emotions, this is the skill to work on first. A person needs to understand why it doesn't make sense to wallow in jealousy: If you have chosen this path together, the presence of another person in your partner's life is not a threat to your relationship. Perhaps ironically, it can be used to enrich the primary relationship.

It helps to be emotionally invested in your partner's joy by imagining how it can benefit you. Sharing your positive experiences and affirming the strength of your relationship are all part of supporting your partner's feelings and concerns. And most importantly, support each other through jealous moments by addressing the feeling with love and gentleness. Always listen without judgment. Avoid criticism, contempt, defensiveness, and stonewalling.

Using Compersion
Instead of being threatened or feeling upset when your partner romantically or sexually interacts with another, cultivate compersion. It will bring you a feeling of happiness or sympathetic joy for him/her. Or you might feel excitement for him/her while they are experiencing someone else. This all comes down managing your emotions. We all have emotions and feelings and none of us can avoid that.

Here are some important pointers on how to deal with your emotions:
• Be honest with yourself about how you feel.
• Don't judge yourself for your feelings.
• If your feelings are big, take note of them but shake them off. You get to choose how to think and feel.
• Notice if you have more than one feeling. It may be that you feel

jealous but you are also slightly turned on. Feed the wolf that you want to feed. Lean into the turn-on and see where it takes you.

- Communicate openly. What you feel may be completely different than what your partner is feeling.
- Make sure you create a safe space where you both can be vulnerable. You don't have to agree with your partner, but you will need to create space to allow your partner to express him/herself.
- Find peace, joy and compassion within yourself. If you think your relationship is rocky or unpredictable, then that is what you will create. There will be tension.
- Model your relationship after other couples whom you admire.

If you make compersion a goal, with time you will be able to feel turned on when your partner is receive pleasure from another. When this happens, you know you have achieved compersion. It may not be permanent, but get curious when you feel it and when you do not.

7) Find your intimacy threshold

We all have an intimacy threshold — the point where a situation is too much for us to engage in either physically or emotionally. It might not take much for someone to reach his/her personal limit. It can be reached quickly, without warning and needs to be honored and respected. Remember when Maggie needed to leave the first play party filled with strangers? This party was far beyond her intimacy threshold.

This is when it is extremely important to communicate with your partner. Sometimes it's enough just to take a little break from the action and reconnect with each other. Slow down, and express your fears and boundaries. Sometimes feelings arise when we get something in our heads that begins to overwhelm us. We really need to stay engaged and present with our partner during this time. This feeling can also be reached when watching our partner/spouse engage with others. Are they kissing too passionately, are they spending too much time with them, is he really licking her ass right now? This is a good time to have subtle signals or safe words that can be used to express your partner's attention to your discomfort. A temper tantrum doesn't work but finding the time to communicate honestly with your partner does. Again, everyone has different tolerance levels and it is important to express, acknowledge and respect them.

8) Avoid attachments with others

Unless you are seeking a polyamorous relationship, be careful of getting too close. Your only relationship should be with your spouse or partner, otherwise, there is likely to be challenges between you or the new addition. You don't want the other couple's husband to be your best friend.

Keep your social time and playtime as a foursome, if they are a couple. This will serve you better in the long run. We advise you to keep your playtime as just playtime. This will avoid things from going down the wrong road.

Be mindful of your communications. We have found it best if texts or email threads include everyone so there is no confusion and keeps everyone up to date with the discussion.

Josh - There were two couples whom we met on a cruise ship that appeared quite close to each other. They were friends that traveled together on all their adult vacations. One day, a new couple asked one of the couples if they would like to dine together. They said yes, so the four of them had dinner together that night. Unfortunately, it did not go well with their other friends. It was apparent there was some jealousy involved and the other friends felt left out. This dynamic showed us that jealousy and control can happen even between couples, not just individuals.

9) Share your experience

The deeper connection you have with your partner, the more fun you will have in the Lifestyle. After playtime, we always talk about the experience we just had. (The "Don't Kiss and Tell" rule definitely doesn't apply to info sharing between couples.) Did the other couple connect? How did they perform? Orally? Kissing? Fucking? Did they make your partner cum multiple times? Was there anything offensive or off-putting about them? Did you get their number? Should you introduce them to your other play friends? This is an important way for you to stay connected with your beloved one.

10) Be secure in your skin

We all have insecurities and body issues at certain times of our lives. We've been to Lifestyle parties and felt it. We would look over at a hot couple who were younger, taller, prettier and fitter. This could make us feel uncomfortable in our own skin. But as Roosevelt once said, "Comparison is the thief of joy," and we were on a path to experience more joy.

Josh and I needed to build our self-confidence so we could feel secure about who we were. This self-confidence is what others began to notice about us. This wasn't easy in the beginning because we were on display, fully naked for all to see. With age came wisdom and the realization that we were not just our bodies.

How we felt about who we were is what we projected to others. What we realized was everyone looked beautiful and sexy as long as they showed confidence and self-love.

Maggie - Most people seemed critical of themselves; even the most beautiful couples we know would talk about things they wished were different about themselves. Thankfully, we are not all built the same.

For years in my 40s, I would put my body through a whole ordeal in preparation for a week-long Lifestyle trip. I would check my period schedule and if it didn't line up with the trip, I would adjust it by doubling up on the Pill or I would stop it early and change the menstrual cycle. How insane was that? The checklist seemed endless...I would do extreme diets just to lose another five pounds prior to leaving for the trip. I would book Botox treatments and a dozen tanning sessions right up to the day we were leaving. I would get my teeth whitened and body wraps to get rid of my cellulite. I figured that if I was desirable physically, I could have more sexual encounters.

As I grew more spiritually, I realized that I was not just my body. I was beautiful inside and outside and the people with whom I wanted to connect would notice.

11) Practice the "Safer Sex Elevator Pitch"

We know practicing safer sex minimizes the risk of pregnancy and STI transmission. For most of us, this boils down to wearing condoms during penetrative activities. You may also choose to carry out lower-risk activities like manual sex/masturbation. You will want to talk to your new playmate about it before getting naked together.

You are "fluid bonded" with everyone with whom you have unprotected sex that shares bodily fluids. Make sure that you know and trust those whom you allow into this inner circle. Just because you are playing with a couple, doesn't mean that they are safe. Remember, Swingers are pleasure-seeking humans and not all of them practice safe sex so it's imperative to keep you and your partner safe by mitigating risks.

Volunteer information and ask questions. I know this topic can be a buzzkill, a red flag, or a signal of distrust, but don't think of it like that. Some of you may feel embarrassed and this could lead to rejection but it is a chance we recommend taking. The more you talk about it with others, the more comfortable you will be. Talking about safer sex is the key to having an open relationship.

Sex educator Reid Mihalko has a two-minute safer sex elevator pitch that he recommends:

1) When were you last tested for STIs? What were you tested for and what were the results?

2) What is your current relationship status and sexual orientation? Single? Married? Poly? Open? Bisexual? Heterosexual? Homosexual? And what agreements do you have with the other person that I should know about?

3) What are your Safer Sex Protocols and needs?

4) Tell me a couple of things you like sexually or want to do with me.

5) What is the one thing you don't like sexually or are not into doing with me today?

6) Have you done any risky sexual things since last being tested? This last question is hotly debated as you are expecting an aroused stranger to tell the truth in front of their partner (who may or may not know all of their sexual activities). This may be trusting a stranger too much.

7) Allow the other person to share the same info.

12) Respect consent at all times

Consent is mandatory at all times for all genders. Ask before you touch. Never assume you are invited into anyone's personal or physical space. NO means no. Maybe means no. Silence means no. Sure can express ambivalence. Only a clear concise YES means yes. Consent can also be revoked at any time.

See people getting it on? That's between them, and because they have consent from each other. Don't watch or jump into anyone's play without asking first. Also, consent can change from one party to another party. So don't take it personally if someone changes their mind.

If you're struggling with consent, check out the "Tea Consent" video on YouTube. This will teach you everything you need to know about consent. "Consent is everything."

Hesitation is another way of saying No!
- Josh

NB. When you take out a camera at a party, private or otherwise, always ensure that everyone present consents to his/her photo being taken. Also, obtaining consent applies to unsolicited touch, even at an orgy. Always ask first. Sometimes our partners give "blanket consent" when having sex and this allows us to go with the flow and follow our inspiration. If there's something he/she doesn't like, they tell us.

13) Be mindful of adding singles to your playtime

You may feel you need to institute a different set of guidelines for Unicorn/Bull play. Your agreement may be that playtime must be with all three of you together in the same room, or if playing separately, it might be limited somehow. We restrict this type of play to only once or twice a month so that the single friend doesn't get too familiar and the playtime together remains special. It can also heighten the anticipation of your next encounter. This single person has a life outside of your and your partner's lives. Let him/her live it. It is not your place to be demanding. Let them date whomever they want.

Discuss your intentions. You can have playtime, but keep your emotions in check. Sometimes there can be a bit of jealousy and hard feelings especially if the person is younger, prettier, tighter, bigger cock, etc. This will only make your spouse feel secondary and insecure about your relationship. Remember, you are committed to your partner. He/she is your beloved one whom you love unconditionally.

Your partner has always been there for you. Don't mess that up. Some singles end up falling in love with their new play friends, and they want more. This feels great for your ego, but this is where you, as a committed couple, must create and stick with your boundaries with your single lover.

Polyamory is a completely different arrangement and there are deeper emotions and commitments between all partners. There are plenty of resources out there if you are interested in this relationship model.

14) Bring on the multiple men

Sex with multiple male partners has its own special rewards and complications. Some single men in the Lifestyle have a tendency to be a bit more aggressive or dominant in their roles. Gang bangs are a good example of this with the woman being the receiver. It can be very satisfying for her if it fulfills a domination or rape fantasy but she still remains in total control.

Performance anxiety is a topic of concern...and may be aggravated by the presence...for many men in the Lifestyle and may be compounded by the presence of another man. Having more than one male in the room also can lead to competitiveness between the men. If the guys can get over the idea of crossing swords or seeing another man naked in close proximity, an extra appendage provides some additional input for the women. However, any insecurities may hinder performance.

Some of the fun ways to enjoy a penis parade include Double Vaginal Penetration or DVP. This is having two cocks in the pussy at the same time. Double Penetration or DP is having one cock in the pussy and another cock in the ass. An Airtight is accomplished with one cock in each hole: vagina, ass, and mouth. These can all feel amazing but can be difficult to perform. You should feel very comfortable and have a good sense of humor with all your play partners. And of course, you need at least three cocks for a gang bang!

15) Multiple women, multiple O's

The sexual wise woman, Jacqueline Hellyer, describes sexual energies this way: "The masculine is like fire — it ignites rapidly, burns brightly and extinguishes quickly; the feminine is more like water — it's slow to heat up but once up to temperature it can boil and boil" ...with multiple orgasms. Thus, playtime with multiple women has its own unique passion and flow. The feminine energy tends to create a very sensual and erotic atmosphere building over a period of time. We often play with a single woman because of this. Josh and I enjoy the energy that it brings to the scene and the passion and intimacy between us are heightened. A high proportion of the women we have met in the Lifestyle have a bisexual or bi-curious aspect to them. This community provides them with a way to explore their sexuality in a safe and inviting arena.

Creating a sorority of women can debunk the standard framework of competition and instill feelings of a hot, sexy sisterhood. You must be mindful of the energy that you are bringing to these relationships. Uplift your sisters.

16) Experiment with toys and props

Not everyone is into the plastic fantastic, but toys can add an extra dimension to your sexual pleasure. Talk to your partner to see if it is something that interests him/her. Some guys find them offensive or think that the tools are just a replacement for the real thing. For us, they are an enhancement to the natural flesh and bone(rs).

One popular piece of equipment is the Sybian, a ride-on toy, made for personal pleasure. Imagine a small ottoman with a dildo attachment on the seat and a remote for power and vibratory control. We have been to a number of parties where the girls take turns riding this "fucking bronco" much to the cheers and encouragement of the spectators. And if a guy likes anal play, it works for him too.

If you haven't visited a sex shop lately, there are thousands of options that might light a new fire in your sex life: electro-stimulation systems, floggers, ropes for bondage, butt plugs, chastity devices... the list is almost limitless. It is your decision whether you want to add these new ingredients to your sex life, but if you do, it will increase the options for what is on the menu. We find that a variety of toys spices up our playtime with the two of us and with others. Variety is the spice of life.

Maggie- The ship's next destination was a full day sail from where we departed. The trip organizers always had plenty of entertainment lined up to keep us from getting bored on these occasional days at sea. But that wasn't enough for us. To fill the time one afternoon a new couple whom we met suggested we join them in their stateroom for some afternoon delight. She was hot for me and wanted to share her double-ended Feeldoe, a vibrating strapless double dildo. It had a penis shape on one end and a bulbous side that was inserted into the vagina on the other. She lay down on her back and slid the bulbous portion inside of herself and then invited me to slide the other end inside as I straddled her hips. The guys watched in awe as we moved and positioned our bodies so the toy would reach the perfect spots. There was so much stimulation that I came fast and hard. The combination of visual, audible and physical sensations brought me to a full-body shaking orgasm very quickly. It was so much fun we ordered our own when we got back home.

17) Have fun with Unicorns and Stunt Cocks

The hosts of many couple's play parties invite single women (Unicorns) and men along to join in the fun. We call the men "Stunt Cocks" — a reference to the film industry's "stunt double," or a stunt man that covers for an actor in physically demanding stunts. Similarly, when playtime begins, there may be extra men invited to wait in the wings until participation is requested. Most women can cum many more times than most men, so having the extra standby dick can be really helpful to satisfy the women's needs.

The role of the Stunt Cock is to wait for a woman to invite them into the playtime. Popular stunt cocks are not aggressive nor pushy. They know their roles. They are typically real gentlemen. Generally, they wait until the other men need a break then they come in and continue to pleasure the women.

Unicorns are sexy, single women in the Lifestyle, a rare and treasured magical beast. By definition, they are bisexual and are in huge demand, but very short supply. Because of the high percentage of Bi-females, they often attend play parties and Lifestyle events looking for a match. Some can also come attached to couples in a poly arrangement or are just there for sexual fun. These women feel comfortable and accepted in this safe environment. We have not experienced a Lifestyle event that did not accept single ladies to attend whereas the single men need to be sponsored or attend on a specific night.

With the right agreements, great fun can be had with these generous singles.

18) Consider renting a partner

Because most Lifestyle cruises, takeovers and clubs don't allow single men to attend by themselves, a popular solution is sponsorship. Couples that choose this route are responsible for their spouse for the evening or event. This keeps the creep factor to a minimum.

The other way around this is for a single man to find someone that can fill the "spouse" role, albeit temporarily. This doesn't mean that there is necessarily a financial transaction between the couple but there is some benefit that they each get out of their interim relationship. It could be friendship, the offer of travel, or just an attractive person to have on the arm.

Typically the guy is much older than the woman, although we have witnessed it the other way around. If it is the former scenario she is usually young, tight, and beautiful. In many situations the guy doesn't play or has little interaction with others, he just likes to watch his partner with another couple or a Unicorn. For us, one downside to this type of couple is the lack of chemistry between them. So far, we have never found enough of a connection with these types of couples to engage in play. Although, if the guy wants to watch us play with the woman alone we might be into it!

19) Keep your spouse on your radar

When playing with more than just your partner, be careful not to ignore your significant other or let him/her feel abandoned. It is very easy to get so caught up in the moment with someone else that you lose track of time or lose awareness of what is going on in the room. Jealousy can creep in if your partner feels they are being neglected. Eye contact, a gentle touch, and a little smile directed at your partner helps to acknowledge his/her presence and can be just the reassurance that is needed. We frequently check in with each other, sometimes just to make sure we are staying hydrated.

20) Be careful with Newbies who want to play

Advice columnist, Dan Savage, has a "Campsite Rule" that also applies to playing with Newbies: "In any relationship, but particularly those with a large difference of age or experience between the partners, the older or more experienced partner has the responsibility to leave the younger or less experienced partner in at least as good a state (emotionally and physically) as before the relationship."

If you are new to non-monogamy, it may be best to start your play with people who are more experienced than you. If you are experienced, remember the Campsite Rule with regards to Newbies.

Consider these questions: How new is he/she? Has he/she played with couples previously? Has he/she taken your Lifestyle as an open invitation for free sex? Is this Newbie a close friend? How do you deal with this?

If possible, let the female/wife talk privately together with the Newbie, it is less threatening than the male energy. Let them know that you will gladly share your partner with him/her, but express your guidelines and agreements with your partner. Maybe it's okay for this Newbie to play with your partner while you are off playing with another single Swinger. Or maybe you and your partner always play together in the same room. You and your partner decide the rules and abide by them.

Be honest with him/her. State your intentions and discover his/hers. The Newbie needs to honor your arrangements. This person could easily disrupt your relationship with your spouse/partner. Make sure you let the Newbie know that this may be a one-time thing. No attachments, no private texts, no sneaking for extra playtime.

If the person expressing interest in exploring the Lifestyle is a close friend, suggest he/she engages in their first playtime with a couple they don't know or know casually. That way there will be no loss of friendship between you and the Newbie if things go well. There should be no reason for private calls or texts, everyone should be communicating at the same time. As mentioned, we use group texts because they include everyone in the conversation.

21) Use good sex etiquette

The thought of going down on sloppy seconds can turn most people off really fast. It can happen whenever there are multiple partners in a play situation. When you have been playing with one person and then move on to another, be polite and excuse yourself to do a little cleanup on your intimate bits. The next person may not want to taste the remnants of cum on breasts or other body parts. The scent of a well-used pussy on your face might be a big turn-on for you, but may not be for the next woman you kiss, especially if she isn't into women.

Maggie - Josh and I were at a house party and two sexy men were flirting with me. We joined one of the guys, Aaron, and his wife, Beth, for a quickie play session to start the night. Later that evening, I asked the other sexy guy if he and his wife would be interested in hooking up. His response caught me by surprise. He asked me, "Did you fuck my friend Aaron earlier?" When I responded, "Yes," he replied, "I don't do sloppy seconds." I had never heard anyone say that to me before, but I realized that some people are funny that way. If they can't have you in the first round, then they don't want you at all. For some people, this could be one of their rules.

22) Create a connection with the other couple

This is really important. Don't enter the Lifestyle thinking that it's going to be a sexy free-for-all. You are building a four-way connection between you, your partner and another couple. Make a connection through kindness, sincerity and intelligent concern.

If you thought it was tough to hook up with someone when you were single, you'll probably find it's harder when you are Swinging as a couple. Guys, connect with the male half of the other couple and show respect for each other. The same goes for women. For this connection to feel right with everyone, there needs to be a level that is comfortable and trustworthy. Knowing a little bit about your prospective play partner can alleviate many concerns.

We have met couples that were NASA scientists, professors, city workers, Mormon missionaries, CIA agents, actors, professional athletes, and senior government officials. Those couples weren't there to talk about work. The Lifestyle was their escape.

There will be those few couples with whom you feel a real connection. They can become your friends. Just follow your own instincts. So many of the couples who are now in our tribe are ones that we met at Lifestyle events.

23) Create a secret signal

Verbally expressing your wants or interest in another person is an important way for you to communicate with your partner. Sometimes you may not be within earshot so another solution is required. One way that we communicate our desire is to send a non-verbal signal to each other, indicating our interest in someone. Josh and I would arrive at a party and begin "shopping" as we called it. Sometimes we would get separated in the room and our best way to communicate with each other would be to rub our eyeteeth with our thumb and forefinger. One day, a friend of ours noticed what we were doing and said, "You two look like you're vampires sharpening your teeth and getting new couples to join your cult." We laughed at the remark but corrected him saying, "Cults use coercion and control. We don't."

Our signal was a way for us to communicate our interest in someone. The other could then check him/her out and see if there was a sexual attraction. If there was, we would approach the couple to see if they had an interest in connecting with us. A few of our friends have now begun their own practice of non-verbal communication when they are out "shopping." This form of connecting is a great way to express your desires and see if they align with your partner's fancies.

24) Don't judge a book by its cover

Everyone has their checklist of what they want in another couple. It is very rare for both of you to find 100% attraction to another couple: Full physical attraction, full chemistry, full perfection, there is rarely such a thing. Be realistic with your expectations.

The Lifestyle has plenty of unequal couples in terms of what you may judge to be attractive. Sometimes you just need to have a conversation with the person and their beauty starts to shine. They may be incredible lovers, really funny, or there may be many qualities that make them attractive.

Remember the old saying, "Don't judge a book by its cover?" Open yourself up to meet as many couples as possible. Just because you're friendly to them doesn't mean that you have to sleep with them.

When it comes to the Internet, some people are not skilled at creating a good online presence. Look for common interests. Find a good vibe with the other couple; they will be looking for the same.

You never need to settle for something that you truly don't want. It is better to skip the sex than feel ashamed or guilt-riddled because of your choice to have sex with someone with whom you don't feel an attraction. Never "take one for the team" and have sex with a couple only because of your partner's desires. This will lead to resentment.

25) Communicate your boundaries, fears and desires

Once a connection is made, the communication needs to be transparent between the couples. If you are with another couple or a single, make sure that you are all on the same page. This is an important time to talk about each person's boundaries, fears and desires. Once these three topics have been discussed (before taking any mind-altering drugs/alcohol), everyone involved feels a lot more comfortable. This dissolves tension and makes playtime much more enjoyable.

We all have our boundaries, those lines in the sand that should not be crossed. It could stem from past trauma, personal beliefs, or agreements with your partner. Everyone's boundaries are different and they need to be established for everyone's comfort. Fears/concerns could evolve from past experiences or feeling the loss of control. Desires, or personal yearnings, may often be the most difficult one to express, especially if you have shame around sexual desires. Give each other space to express these feelings and accept them without judgment.

A lack of communication leaves too much room for the imagination - Sangram Keshari

26) Allow the ladies to lead

Swinging is not a sexual free-for-all where people live hedonistically without consequence. As mentioned, the Lifestyle requires careful decision-making, checking in with your partner regularly, and plenty of steamy consensual sexploration! In the early phase, the man may screen for potential contacts, especially online, but the woman has the veto power.

As a woman, my comfort level was much greater once I understood that I had the power to initiate and veto those with whom I would be intimate. I would open a line of trust with the other female by finding out what she was into and what her boundaries were. Women want to be listened to and made to feel special. I like finding the thing about another woman that *is* special.

Another side of allowing the ladies to lead is the practice by men in the Lifestyle that ensures that their partners are satisfied before turning to their own personal gratification. If they can't arrange for simultaneous orgasms, good male partners in the Lifestyle are true gentlemen and have the spirit of, "I insist, after you..." if that's the case.

27) Raising the flag on the play

The middle of playtime is not when your rules or agreements should be changed. But, sometimes the situation requires you to raise a flag on the play. It could be an emotion that came up or some other discomfort. If that's the case you may want to have a signal between you and your partner. Maybe a special wink, a particular gesture or a special word between each of you. Come up with a code word or signal that you both will understand clearly.

We can all find ourselves in an uncomfortable place and feel the need to pull back or flee. Or maybe the agreements that you have made with your partner are not being honoured. This can cause confusion and mistrust and can kill the mood of all people involved. There won't be any regrets if you follow your own rules or intuition. Review the situation in private later and discuss if it is something that needs to be added to these agreements.

Remember when I called the playtime when The Captain was making lewd advances? Josh instantly agreed to leave when I raised the flag on the play.

28) Find yourself a mentor

It is good to have a go-to person that can help you navigate the many directions the Lifestyle offers. If you need such a person, Josh and I will be offering coaching and seminars to guide you and your partner in your exploration of non-monogamy. Look for the details in the Resource section at the back of the book.

Don't be afraid to ask questions and ask for pointers in your relationship with your partner or playmates. If something doesn't feel right for you or your partner, then it is time to talk about it and set new ground rules.

Aside from mentors, the Internet has a wealth of knowledge that may help guide you along the way. Online discussion groups are great resources since the comments come from so many different perspectives. However, this is your journey and your relationship so only you know your desires and limitations. Once again, communication is of utmost importance.

As mentioned in our book, I met our mentor at one of our very first Lifestyle events. The couple was really well known in the Lifestyle community and had been active for many years. Both of them had open, confident personalities with zero drama. Josh and I looked up to their commitment and support of each other's pleasure. They had experience and were gracious in sharing their knowledge with us. They invited us to the right parties, introduced us to some wonderful people, exposed us to unique Lifestyle travel destinations, and told us which websites to check out. This help gave us the confidence to continue our adventure.

If you need a mentor, Josh and I offer our experience to aid you in your own journey.

Check out our website at: www.evolutionarysex.org.

29) Re-evaluate your agreements when needed

The rules that you set when you first start exploring the Lifestyle are bound to change. We have known many couples over the years that began their journey with Soft Swing or strictly girl-on-girl. When we saw them a few years later they were into full-on gang bangs and kink. It isn't usually that extreme, but do be prepared to have on-going discussions about your comfort level. Be respectful of your partner's feelings and desires. Check in regularly with him/her and see if there are any adjustments that need to be addressed in your agreements.

30) Set up a well-developed online profile

The world has changed considerably since Josh and I got into the Lifestyle. In the early days, the Internet was rather limited and many couples still used the want ads in alternative newspapers. Since then, Lifestyle-focused websites have popped up in all regions. As founding members of a few of these sites, we have seen phenomenal growth in the memberships. One site keeps us up to date with the lo-cal scene, another site we use for international travel, and another helps us remain in touch with the hundreds of people we have met over the years.

Whichever site you feel most attracted to, remember that it requires "self-marketing" to attract others to your profile. Think about what you look for when checking out others. Unless your genitals are ex-tremely unique, your cock or pussy shot won't get much attention. Remember, the ladies lead and most women don't love cock or pussy shots. You don't need many pictures but include at least one full -body dressed and one naked/nearly naked. Other things to consider are:
• Keep the pictures current, we have been surprised more than once to discover the photos on profiles were 10 years and 30 pounds dif-

ferent. Immediately, this creates an atmosphere of dishonesty.

- Definitely include photos of the male half of the couple.
- Clean up the background before you take the photo. We won't be moving in with you but if you live in a mess, your life might be a mess too.
- Be sexy and show off your wild side in the photos.
- Show off what you like best about yourself. Nice ass? Then show it off! It is good for the confidence level.
- If you are concerned with anonymity, most Lifestyle sites have the provision for multiple layers of photo access: The first layer can be seen by most, the second layer you can restrict to friends or membership levels, and the third level is restricted to only your pre-approved pass holders.
- If you aren't confident or able to take quality photos, consider hiring a photographer to shoot a boudoir scene. This is a good opportunity to get both of you in the picture. A good photographer will not only make you look sexy but feel it as well.
- Before you write your profile, sit down with your partner and fill out the website's questionnaire together. The questions that are asked are a great way to openly discuss your play preferences with each other.
- Write a paragraph or two that describes you and your play preferences. If you are just starting out and are only comfortable with soft swings, make sure you put that in your profile.
- Be honest. It's OK to be a Newbie, but say so.
- Remember this is sales and marketing. You are the product.
- Some of the sites we are on include: Lifestylelounge.com, Kasidie. com, clubeden.com, llvclub.com. There are sites for virtually every taste and interest.

31) Meet couples at sexy seminars or workshops

This is a great place to meet new friends. Most of the takeovers and large events that we have attended have special guests sharing their knowledge at workshops during the day. As mentioned, the ones that Josh and I have attended include: learning to squirt, how to give the perfect blow job, how to enjoy anal sex, how to pole dance, techniques for Japanese *shibari* rope bondage, kink play and more. These events are always well attended and you know the people who are there also have an interest in the subject.

Whenever we go to those week-long events, we try to attend as many of these workshops as possible. Even if we have been to them before, there is always something new to learn. We can please our lovers by learning a new approach or technique. There may be an opportunity to talk to couples and make a connection for a possible play date, and it might happen immediately as a way to practice your newfound skills. Remember to step out of your comfort zone.

32) Control your expectations or fantasies

You may have several fantasies about going to a play party or date, but make sure you check them at the door. You don't want to be disappointed because of your unfulfilled expectations. Be open to the experience, be present, stay connected to your partner, and go with the flow. That's when the sex magic happens.

Live in the moment. If you are completely present, you can let your inspiration in the moment lead you in your playtime with your spouse and others. You will be able to pick up on the cues from others, and make suggestions for possible play that will be received with excitement. If your suggestions aren't received well, let the flow lead another way. It is not rejection, just the voicing of another person's preferences.

There are so many different types of play: Sport-Fucking, BDSM, kink play, Soft Swing, Full Swing, Neo-Tantra, etc. Always ask the couple beforehand what they are into to avoid awkward surprises. By toning down your preconceived notions of what you think will or should happen, you can enjoy the moment for what it is.

With Internet dating, it's a good idea to meet a new couple at a bar for drinks first. This will give everyone a chance to get to know each other and see if there is any spark. They may have changed their appearance since posting their picture — you dreamed of a redhead and you got a blonde. You might find the guy hot and the woman frigid, or the woman is sweet and sexy and the guy is overbearing. Let these discoveries happen at a low investment location, one where you can make an easy escape. We have found that we don't make dinner dates because two hours with a couple could be ninety minutes too long. We can figure out if the other couple is a good match pretty quickly.

33) Protect yourself

As touched on with the Safer Sex Elevator Pitch, always use condoms. At the sex parties, there would be a stash of condoms and lube next to every bed. Be responsible...respect yourself, your spouse, and your play partner enough to use them!

So many times we have heard guys whining and complaining that the condom was uncomfortable, too tight, too loose, and prevented them from feeling anything. Then there are the ones that have "allergies" to latex but don't seem come supplied with non-latex alternatives. Whatever you do, don't let any man, except the one(s) whom you are committed to and fluid bonded with, persuade you into going bareback. Do you know his medical history? Has he shown you his STI results? Even with clean results, there is no guarantee he's been safe since the test. You have a responsibility to yourself and your partner to stay safe. If the guy wants to ejaculate but finds doing so difficult when he's wearing a condom, you could suggest he pulls out, pulls the condom off, and faps one-off. If it's your thing, allow him to release his load somewhere safe.

34) Mind your personal grooming

From fully waxed to bushy beavers, we've seen them all. Whatever your body hair preferences, remember to keep it clean. Not many like to eat from a hairy plate. Most Lifestylers who we have encountered are either fully shaved or well trimmed but if you like a bush, then wear it proudly. There is always someone who will find that enticing.

Do your partner(s) a favor — don't eat heavy spices, garlic, escargot, Caesar salads, dairy (if it doesn't agree with you), and beans before playtime. You will likely be making a connection with others by close talking, whispering and French kissing. If you're a smoker and you'd like to connect with non-smokers, make sure you brush your teeth and wash your hands after a cigarette. Non-smokers have made the choice to not smoke, so most don't enjoy the taste or the smell of cigarettes.

Wear deodorant and go light on perfumes and aftershaves. When this is mixed with sweat it becomes pungent and a real turn-off. It may be true that your partner loves the smell of your natural body odor, but guaranteed, strangers will not feel the same way.

If you like having your toes sucked, then get pedicures. And that's for the men too!

Maggie - Josh and I were invited to a friend's holiday house in Arizona along with two other couples. We knew all the couples from previous playtimes and were delighted to share an evening of wine and social time.

One of the guys, Dean, expressed an interest in playing with me alone. Our spouses were in agreement so we left the poolside and found ourselves a free bedroom. He began by burying his head in my pussy but it felt, uncomfortable. I pulled away from him and saw the culprit — his new goatee. I explained to Dean that his goatee had a rough and scratchy texture and it was irritating my vaginal lips. I expressed my desire for oral pleasure but I asked him if he would be willing to shave. He must have wanted me badly but suggested we get approval from his wife.

We found the balcony that overlooked the pool. As we stood there naked, he called down to his wife, "Eve, would you mind if I shaved my goatee?" Of course, the others that were there provided some fun-hearted jabs at us. Eve gave her approval but left the final decision to him. His mind was obviously made up so he and I quickly went and shaved it off.

There was an interesting dynamic of power, submission and desire that night. I acknowledged that I had a great deal of control of the playtime and a responsibility not to take advantage of a man's untamed sexual hunger. I did anyway and he loved it. It was one of my powerplays.

35) Be respectful of the play space

If you know you sweat a lot, then bring a towel. I am not a big fan of having a guy on top, sweating profusely on my face so that I have to reposition myself to avoid the sweat falling.

If you know you are a squirter, bring a towel or waterproof blanket or pads. Soaking the linens with your squirting fluids won't make the sheets very comfortable for anyone who has to sleep on the bed later. And please don't forget to pick up your used condoms and wrappers and dispose of them properly. We can't count how many splouge filled bags we've seen left for someone else to dispose of. Ewww!

Remember that Burner principle...Leave no trace.? It's a good life rule. The only traces you want to leave are the good ones...the memories of how much fun you were.

36) Create your community

You will find that as you navigate the Lifestyle, you will naturally find partners who are at your comfort level.

After the initial phase of exploration, Josh and I found that once a friendship between couples was established, we often stuck close to them, at least for a while. Those friends introduced us to other friends and eventually, we had a small community of people who had similar interests and play styles.

Now, our play friends are from all over the world, a combination of people we have met through others, at local events, online and through international adult-only Lifestyle travel. We have known many of our play friends for over twenty years and continue to share great times with them. Something that has changed for us in the last few years is the type of relationship we have. Sex has become a secondary or bonus part of our relationships. It is an indicator that our level of play has changed.

Not all couples that hang around the Lifestyle have sexual interactions with others. These "Soft Swingers" are frequently attracted to others that have adopted that play style. They enjoy the freedom of expression and open, flirtatious communication, but prefer to keep the sex between spouses.

2 x 2 relationships (two couples) can also work really well, especially if the two sets of fantasies and sexual appetites are complimentary. Since some couples rely on this model exclusively, and it is known as "friends-first Swinging," the word friends is the key. If two couples do become romantically involved, then it really isn't Swinging anymore — it is polyamory.

37) Don't kiss and tell

You know the expression "Whatever happens in Vegas, stays in Vegas?" Then the mantra "Whatever happens with Swingers stays...in the room." is a good mantra to adopt while Swinging. When people open up their relationship and their legs to you, it is just good manners to keep their confidence between the people in the room. As discussed in Rule #3, whatever happens behind closed doors, stays closed. It is good practice to stay away from the gossip that involves others, even if it makes you feel part of the cool crowd. Stay away from gossips because if they'll do it about others. they will do it with you (and those are not the people with whom you want to get close).

The exception to this rule is if it concerns someone who plays unsafely or in a way that is dangerous to others. These practices need to be addressed with the person involved.

38) Remember, it's Swingers Anonymous

Closely related to the above point of gossiping or sharing about others is the concept of "outing." Aside from jealousy, the worst fear of most Swingers is probably that they will be "outed." Outing is a term used in alternative lifestyle communities. It refers to revealing aspects or details of someone's private life, activities or Lifestyle choice without their explicit consent. This outing may be done unintentionally or otherwise.

In the Lifestyle, it can show up as the non-consensual disclosure of someone's private life details, choices or preferences so be careful when sharing too much information. The act of outing someone is either an act of carelessness or vindictiveness - neither of which is acceptable.

Josh and I know couples who never play in their own city for fear of being outed. These couples only play while away on Lifestyle vacations.

A few points to be conscious of before unintentionally outing someone includes:
• Awareness — a little forethought goes a long way. Think first before saying something.
• Consent — keep others' personal details to yourself. Don't spread

them or share them without explicit consent. Just because someone trusts you does not mean that they trust people whom you know.

• Discretion — if you do discover others' personal details, forget you ever came to those realizations.

• Learn — if you fucked up, no matter how it happened, admit it and apologize. Do not make the same mistake again. The consequences are more important than the intentions no matter how innocent you believe them to be.

• Introductions — Think of the Swinging community as "Swingers Anonymous" and get consent before introducing anyone within the community. If you play with someone whom you feel would be a good match with someone else you know, ask if they would like to be introduced. Never "out" anyone by making non-consensual introductions. Everyone has different comfort levels around the Lifestyle and how it relates to his/her everyday life.

The bottom line is people have the right to share their own stories with whomever they choose, whenever they choose. Despite this book, we still have people with whom we don't tell our story, like elderly parents who wouldn't understand. This sharing would only conflict with their religious worldview and cause them stress so it is better kept private. A good phrase to keep in your back pocket when you're tempted to share a juicy detail is, "That's not my story to share." Then smile and keep your mouth shut.

39) Be on time for the play party

Being fashionably late can be awkward at a play party. If you show up thirty minutes late, you won't have any time to get to know your play friends. The others will definitely be aroused and eager to get started so they probably won't be sitting around waiting for you to show up. It can be tricky to jump into the action midstream. You may find that many of them are already engaged with someone. If you're really late, you'll be like the second string, waiting on the bench for the first string to get played out.

40) It's OK to take a pill (with your Doctor's approval)

We are including this topic as a public service announcement for all the wonderful ladies who are getting the limp end of the stick. There have been many times that after a play party, I would reflect that my partner had difficulty maintaining an erection. It can happen to any penis — too much alcohol, too tired, too much MDMA, too much discomfort, too many birthdays, too much thinking about too many birthdays, etc. No matter what the cause, most of the time it can be remedied by medical technology, like ED medication.

It's no surprise that Viagra or Cialis has a place in the Lifestyle. Especially on week-long events, it can be challenging to keep it up that long. We find ED meds a topic that many men don't like to talk about. It seems to be a direct assault on their masculinity, so it remains a little secret. All we can say is suck it up, talk to your doctor and don't disappoint your play partners.

NB Josh prefers Cialis. It lasts for a few days with him and doesn't cause the stuffy sinus effects of the other brands. And he performs like a porn star!

41) Embrace the changes

My body started to change when I was forty-seven. For a few months, my periods became more frequent and extreme. There was a side of me that was happy for that phase of my life to be over. Never again would I have to worry about getting pregnant, being bloated or enduring crazy mood swings. Never again would I have to worry about my period ruining a playtime with Josh or anyone else.

Josh was really happy about it too. It was a total relief for both of us. Yet, this new life phase brought its own challenges. In menopause, my body roared. I experienced the hot flashes, weight gain, night sweats, joint pain, insomnia and vaginal dryness that are typical. My dripping wet, aroused pussy that I (and others) had always enjoyed had semi-retired and lube was now my best friend.

Even with the new challenges, I discovered that I didn't have to say goodbye to pleasurable and satisfying sex. As I approached my change of life, I found an ND (Naturopathic Doctor) that was up-to date on hormone replacement therapy. I began taking progesterone daily and added weekly vaginal estrogen cream to prevent dryness and thinning of the vaginal walls. I adjusted my diet, reduced my alcohol intake and exercised more. By keeping my body balanced, my sex drive was maintained and I could continue to enjoy the pleasures I desired.

I took a step back in my career, let my children figure out their own lives, and had more me time. This was a new chapter in my life and I was going to embrace it.

If and when you or someone you love experiences menopause, I advise searching for a qualified hormone specialist in your area. They can help you keep your libido high by balancing your hormones. They can also recommend lifestyle changes, but don't think that you have to change your decision to be in the Lifestyle, just because of your collection of birthdays.

42) Aim to please and don't be a lazy lover

Most of us want to bring pleasure to our partners, especially in the bedroom. Be aware of the feedback loop by being present and paying attention to the responses that your touch provides. This will help you discover your lover's erogenous zones. Having a mutual masturbation session and watching how your partner self-pleasures is a great way to discover preferences. Open up a conversation and listen as he/she shares the techniques that bring on that mind-blowing, toe-curling orgasm. Your reward will be knowing that you have satisfied him/her. Let your motto be, "I aim to please."

Just because you know how to play the piano, doesn't mean you know how to play the oboe. Likewise, every person is different with regard to what turns him/her on. You may know what pleases your partner (and we hope you do), it may take only the smell of your panties for him to get hard, but don't assume those things will please the new person in front of you. As mentioned, learn to be a good listener and listen to the feedback loop of sounds of pleasure. If you have someone who is particularly silent (and this happens) use your words to encourage conversation around what he/she likes and doesn't like.

On the receiving end, lying with your back to the mattress and expecting another to do all the work to please you is not only selfish but it doesn't do anything to encourage a lover to satisfy your needs. Be proactive — express your desires or at least put yourself in a position that communicates your intentions. Vocalize your pleasure: Moans and groans inform your partner of your arousal and trigger your own deeper, sexual sensations.

With good sex, there is no real differentiation between giving and receiving. They both will be equally enjoyable. Be equally engaged when giving as receiving. Accept the attention from your playmate as a gift and your appreciation and presence are the gift you return to them. Josh and I find great joy in feeling and hearing our play partners in ecstasy.

Maggie - One evening Josh and I were invited to a couple's stateroom for a play session. The couple was extremely hot and ready to perform. She was known as an "Insta-squirter" — she just had to fantasize about a man, and she would squirt.

It could be that because she was so easily satisfied, her husband never really learned that some women require, and enjoy, much more attention. He must have thought that I would be just like his wife and instantly cum, but just a couple of kisses on my pussy did not get me off. Either he couldn't read the room, or was just too lazy to read the room, either way he wasn't interested in investing the effort required to satisfy me.

It was a disappointing playtime for me, but from the action that took place on the other side of the bed, Josh left feeling like a superhero.

Josh - This was the first time I had been introduced to a self-proclaimed Tantra instructor and it was well before I had become much more connected to my body and the energetic field in and around me. She was very attractive and had a quiet, confident personality. I was excited at the possibilities of what the sex would be like... new positions, techniques, the way she would touch. What new things would I learn?

It turned out to be underwhelming. I found it difficult to connect with her that day. I learned in that moment how important it was to be present and aware of a partner's desires and play styles, not just as the giver but as the receiver as well.

Since starting our journey into the realm of sex-is-energy, I have often found myself questioning my play styles with new partners. I find I need to consciously stay present and sense the responses I am getting to my touch. Some like it slow and gentle, while others want it fast and hard. And just because a partner likes it slow one day, it doesn't mean that he/ she doesn't want it fast and hard the next.

Presence is essential no matter what kind of play I am involved in, whether it be energetic, kink, BDSM, or straight sex. Maggie and I can lie embraced together for extended periods with little movement and just share energies. It is a wonderful heart-fulfilling time together but could be boring for most playtime with others.

If my partner isn't responding to whichever moves I am using, then I change it up and look and listen for a different response. Sexual satisfaction can sometimes be a moving target and you will need to stay focused to achieve the desired results. Stay present in your activity, now is not the time to be...Squirrel!

43) Go easy on your alcohol and drug intake

So many times, we have seen too much alcohol get messy. The guy gets too drunk and insists that he is good to go and wants some playtime with us. And as he is stripping off his clothes, he takes another shot of "liquid courage" to calm his nerves. Well, that's not all he calms... I am left with his limp dick. Now he's embarrassed and there's awkwardness in the room.

It is easy to get caught up in settling the nerves with alcohol. The effect it can have on our sexual performance (as well as our judgment) are good reasons to limit the intake. And that goes for drugs as well. MDMA can heighten emotions but can also leave a man with a rope, not a staff. Other drugs can make people bounce off the walls, but with a flaccid phallus.

I enjoy ending a playtime session by having intercourse with my partner du jour, but he first needs to rise to the occasion. So I pay attention to whom I choose to play with at a party.

44) Cock-blocking

Cock-blocking is successfully interfering with a person's attempt at having sex. This behavior could be driven by genuine concern for one or more of the people involved. In the Lifestyle community, it is a practice used to protect another female from unwanted advances or actions from an undesirable male.

There are many reasons for not including someone in playtime, the most common being aggression before or during play. Unacceptable touching, verbal abuse or any other offence, are all grounds for blocking. Blocking can manifest as not inviting the guilty person to a party or basically making him feel like a "persona non grata" or unwelcome person. The same situation could arise with a female, we just haven't experienced it.

In our early years of playing, Josh and I were invited to a Lifestyle house party along with ten other couples. At the party, a cute guy asked if I wanted some playtime with him, alone. I talked with Josh and he agreed that I could go into one of the bedrooms by myself with the veritable stranger but I figured that since he and his wife had been invited to the play party, he was pre-screened and he would be a gentleman.

I was wrong. He closed the bedroom door, ripped off our clothes and threw me on the bed. I accepted this as an offside power play but then he pinned me down on the bed and started grinding hard against my body. I had a belly piercing and since he was crushing against me, it was causing the ring to rip my skin. I asked him to slow down and give me a break but then he continued grinding. I finally pushed him off, but he continued kissing me aggressively and biting my lips. He was relentless and had no notion of consent.

Everything about that experience felt uncomfortable and wrong. It made me feel out of control. Luckily, I was able to make an excuse to leave. I got up, grabbed my clothes and went back to the party. But I didn't bring up the situation to anyone at the time. I didn't want to start any drama during the party, I blocked it out and went on with my night.

On the drive home, Josh and I talked about that encounter. He felt very concerned for me but understood why I didn't want to cause any drama while at the party. He knew I could handle myself and would deal with it on my own but it was reassuring to know he was there to back me up.

A few weeks later, we attended another local house play party and the same guy and his wife were invited again. I spoke to some of the women about my experience with him and they echoed that they too had experienced his dominance as well. We came to the decision to cock-block him that evening to protect any unsuspecting woman he might approach.

We were the judge and jury. His aggressive play style wasn't acceptable to our group and we didn't want to make a scene so we dealt with it quietly. This was the last party we ever saw them at. They were officially removed from the guest list.

NB From an evolutionary psychology perspective, this form of gossip is a positive way to "monitor cooperative reputations." It is a way to keep people, especially women, safe.

45) Plan a great play party

To plan a great play party, you must remember to keep your expectations in check. There is no guarantee that there will be naked bodies writhing in ecstasy all over your living room floor. Sometimes the flow of the party doesn't go there for anyone. We have had many parties become purely social events and we still enjoy the evening. Who doesn't like to dress sexy, flirt, and be free to talk about anything (except for religion, politics, or anything polarizing). Don't feel the night wasn't successful just because you didn't get laid.

You will need to decide which type of play party you want to have Will you have a theme? Will you be providing play areas and food? How many people can you accommodate? It's a good idea to attend as many parties as you can before planning your own. This will help you research what makes a party good for you.

No one looks good under LED, halogen, or fluorescent lighting. Begin by setting the mood with low lighting, creating more intimate play areas. At some parties we have attended, the hosts remove all the family photos and redecorate with a sexy theme. Do what feels best for you.

We have hosted or attended many different types of parties over the years. Some have been intimate, others very public. The one commonality to almost all is the existence of a theme. We have hosted kink parties with a guest Dominatrix who provided her toys and demonstrated her skills on our asses. We have rented party buses to drive us around and visit strip clubs. We even hosted an evening of body painting. It was exciting to see all the sexy bodies covered in colorful latex. It was fun peeling it off to reveal our naked skin. (If you do try body paint, we recommend shaving all the little hairs off the body, otherwise, it's like removing Band-Aids.)

We strongly suggest that if you can't be a gracious host, don't be a host at all. If you can't relax and enjoy while others are in your home, you're not the one to have the party. Your guests will feel your tense vibe and it will affect the evening. Find another way to give to your friends and community.

46) Keep it light and fun with sex energy!

We don't go to coffee for our energy. We also don't say we're too tired for sex. Sex energizes not depletes us. We have a list of friends who can recharge our batteries in wonderfully pleasurable ways. Sex should be fun. Be playful, be funny and be lighthearted. Play games, be silly, and find humor in that pussy fart.

Being carefree and playful helps to deepen our feelings of affection and gives us a healthy state of intimacy and connection with our friends. Too many of us let the seriousness of our daily responsibilities carry over into our sexy times. We forget to *chill the fuck out*. Our relationships with our play friends thrive on us having joy and sexual energy together. When we are silly, we notice the tensions dissolve. They reveal sides of themselves that are usually suppressed. Just because we grow older doesn't mean we can't embrace the fun and the joys of our youth.

Joyful playtime helps us create a deeper sense of intimacy and connection by relaxing our inhibitions. It helps us to become energetically charged and alive in the moment. An element of playfulness has always contributed beneficial energy between us which has enhanced our relationship immensely. Even during a very intimate sensual exchange, we often find ourselves pulling back, checking in and lightening up the mood. These little breaks are a good time to drink some water and have a little snack. It's like having recess! (And yes, play sessions should be long enough that you have time for an intermission.)

47) Practice bed notching, or maybe not

The term "bed notched" refers to the practice of tallying the number of sexual partners you've had by putting a mark on your bedpost. The play partners are used as an object to satisfy a sexual desire and nothing more. We admit we were more like that at the beginning, but some couples consider it an Olympic sport.

Maggie - On one of our cruises, Josh and I met a young couple in the nightclub. It was around 1 am and they approached us to ask if we would like to join them in the playroom. We hadn't previously talked to them but they were hot, and we thought it would be fun to end the evening with a bit of a ground and pound.

Once we got to the playroom we chose a bed, disrobed, and got to know each other. It was fast and furious and over in less time than it takes to make (white) rice. After the guys had unloaded their guns, the wife quickly grabbed her clothes and said "I'm going to the bathroom." The three of us continued to chat, but I could tell that the husband was feeling distracted. She was gone for a while when he got up and said, "I better go check on my wife." He grabbed his clothes and walked off. That's when Josh and I realized that this couple was not coming back. We had been "Bed notched." We were now just a statistic in their book of conquests. We laughed about this turn of events. It didn't bother us in any way, in fact, we felt honored. We ran into them later and they greeted us like we were old friends. We didn't bring any awkwardness to the greeting so, it wasn't awkward.

48) Use your sexy words

Have you ever been with a dirty talker? A verbal-porn-scene-playing chatterbox? It can be quite erotic and a real turn-on. Neither Josh nor I are big cussers but a little flirtatious talking always lightens the mood during sex. We often use verbal foreplay like this to turn each other on.

Josh - One of my early playmates took me through a whole storyline one afternoon during our playtime. We were on a cruise ship docked in Trieste, Italy. Across the water from us was a huge, private yacht moored to the opposite dock. Our balcony doors were open and we had a clear view of the deckhands busy cleaning and readying the boat for use. My play friend, Nora, whispered into my ear the things she was going to do to me and the things she wanted me to do to her. Her words were sexy and in graphic detail. She then told a story about the crew on the other ship watching us while we were there, fucking. I wish I could recall everything she said that day, but I was so enthralled and in the moment. She was a walking, talking erotic novel but in 4-D. What a turn-on!

NB Be aware that all words have power and mean different things to different people based on their personal experiences. Consider this, you may find that a woman enjoys calling males, "Daddy" but if you have your own biological children, this may be a complete turn-off in a sexual situation. Be mindful that just because something is hot to you, doesn't mean it is hot to someone else. You may like the word slut, but your play partner may hate it. Be open to experimentation but willing to communicate when something doesn't work for you.

49) Live life shamelessly

We judge others, and more importantly, we judge ourselves. If you have a battle with your desires, chances are you're going to see that as judgments reflected back from the outside world. What can you do to prevent this? Start with yourself.

Know that your desires aren't wrong. Shame comes from the belief that there is something wrong with you. There is nothing wrong with you. Just because you see the world through a different lens, and have desires that are different from the norm, this doesn't make you wrong.

The judgments that many of us have encountered through our families/cultures can prevent us from being true to ourselves. The opinions of others can cause us to act in ways that deny our true natures. When you are brave enough to express your desires openly, you are able to find a tribe of like-minded people. There is *always* someone who shares your kinks or fantasies.

The Lifestyle offers a sexy community of support and understanding. By helping others to express pleasure, we make it easier to celebrate our own. Despite the openness, for many people, the Lifestyle is a secret existence. It is a safe harbor in their life. They keep it that way to avoid the judgment that may be directed at them from others in their community. It is a reason why so many Swinger destinations are successful.

Before we came out to our kids, Josh and I still had secrecy about our lifestyle choices. Why? We didn't want our children to feel the repercussions or judgments from others about our lifestyle. We were shame free about our choices yet we chose to wait until our kids were adults before we shared our open relationship status with them. Since then, we've noticed that our already loving sons have become even more loving and open. The openness is contagious.

"Your heart knows the way, run in that direction".
- Rumi

50) Play by the rules

Josh and I never constrained ourselves with too many rules. One of the ways that we have navigated was to always take the path most pleasurable. Sometimes to create a space for your pleasure, rules must be made. You will discover the ones that work for you. Expect there to be bumps along the way. When this happens, adjustments may be necessary. Experiment with what works for you and your partner. These are what have worked for us:

The top seven on this list (told you it was short):

Rule #1 - Mates before Dates. Connect with your partner

Rule #2 - Ladies first. Women choose the play partners

Rule #3 - Don't kiss and tell

Rule #4 - Practice safe sex

Rule #5 - Never take one for the team

Rule #6 - Always meet each other's play partners before playing

Rule #7 - Always obtain consent - especially before consuming mind altering substances

Congratulations! You now have the access to our wisdom of over twenty years of experience in the Swinger Lifestyle. See you at the next "Meet & Greet!"

May you feel free to express
your erotic pleasures and find your tribe.
May you find a deeper, more honest connection
with yourself and your partner.
And may you "go with the flow" to
create your own Divine sexual journey.
- Maggie and Josh

"Don't be ashamed
of your story
—
it will inspire others."

— Anonymous

Alt Dic - an alternate dictionary

Airtight - the act of putting penises in the vagina, ass, and mouth at the same time

Akashic records - a compendium of all universal events, thoughts, words, emotions and intent ever occurred in the past, present and future

Allosexual - being sexually attracted to anyone, whether gay, lesbian, bisexual, pansexual or any other sexual orientation

Asexual - non-sexual, a person who has no sexual feelings or desires

Ayahuasca - a plant medicine from South America

Bating - a shortened term for masturbating

BDSM - bondage; discipline; Sadomasochism

Bed notching - Keeping track of sexual conquests

Body shots - alcohol poured on a naked body and licked off by others

Bondage - sexual practice involving restraining a partner

Blobby - a blow job that is enjoyable like a hobby

Breath work - controlled breathing during meditation or therapy

Bi/Bisexual - attracted to both men and women

Bull - a guy who is just for casual sex with a partnered female; he may be single or part of a couple.

Butt plug - a sex toy designed to be inserted into the rectum for sexual pleasure

Cock-blocking - a person who unwittingly (out of ignorance) or purposefully (out of jealousy or protection) prevents another person from engaging with members of the opposite sex

Cowboy/cowperson - the partner being penetrated straddles their partner facing them or away (Reverse cowperson).

Cuckold - a man who is aroused by watching his female partner engaging in sex with another man

Compersion - a feeling of joy/happiness (or arousal) for your partner when he/she is experiencing pleasure with a partner other than you

Crossing swords - when two or more guys are having sex with a woman and they accidentally touch penises

Dantian - the seat of life force energy in your body; the energy centre of Chinese medicine

Demisexual - people who experience sexual attraction only after an emotional connection is established

Dildo - an object shaped like an erect penis used for sexual stimulation

DMT - dimethyltryptamine, the "God molecule," naturally occurs in nature and the human body, where it is most prevalent at birth and death; a very strong psychedelic chemical

Dogging - where people meet and watch others having sex in a public place with at least one stranger

Do-overs - having sex with a single or couple for a second time

Dominatrix (Dom/Domme (f)) - opposite of a submissive; it is the person who takes the dominant role in BDSM sexual activities

DP - Double Penetration; having one cock in the pussy and another cock in the ass

DVP - Double Vaginal Penetration; having two cocks in the pussy at the same time.

Edging - a sexual practice of holding off right before the point of male or female ejaculation / orgasm

Erroscia - a sex toy used by females to stimulate the clitoris

Energy orgasm - non-sexual orgasm; physical climax without genital stimulation or ejaculation

Enlightened - knowing your true self/your inner being, aligning with the light

ENM - ethical non-monogamy; the agreement of all partners

Exhibitionism - exposing the genitals to others

Face-sitting - queening; when one person sits on another person's face

Fapping - masturbating

Feeldoe - strapless dildo by Erogenics Inc.

Fetish - a strong liking for a particular object/activity for sexual gratification

Fisting - the act of putting a fist or hand into the vagina or anus

Fire play - in BDSM, various sexual practices involving fire

Fluid - the idea that sexual orientation can change over time, and depends on the situation at hand.

FMF - female/male/female; a threesome with two females and one male

Foursome - a group of four people having sex

Four-way - two couples engaging in sexual activity

Full swing - a couple engaging in every sexual activity with another person or couple

Gang bangs - a group of 3-4 men having sex with a woman (or male in gay situations)

Gay - sexual desire directed toward people of one's own sex/gender aka homosexual

Girl/girl - two women interacting sexually from passionate kissing to "grab the strap-on and giddy up"

Gloryhole - a hole made in a thin wall/partition; the hole where a man can insert his penis for sexual stimulation by an anonymous person on the other side of the wall

Golden shower - urinating on another person for sexual pleasure

Gray sexuality - rarely experience sexual attraction or experience it at a low level

Group play - aka orgy

Guy/guy - two penis owners engage in sexual activity

Hair play - engaging in sensual touching, massaging or pulling of the hair

Hall pass - one of the partners has permission to play on his/her own while away from the other

Hook up - a casual sexual encounter aka one-night stand

Hot husband - a husband who sets up a casual sex date with other women

Hot wife - a wife who sets up casual sex dates with other men.

Kink play - unconventional sex play

Kundalini - a distinct feeling of electric energy running up the spine thru the nerves

Lesbian - a homosexual woman

Lifestyle - open-relationship; non-monogamy, aka Swinger

LTA - living together and apart

MDMA - a psychedelic drug that reduces inhibitions and increases heart connections, aka ecstasy/Molly

MFM - male/female/male; a threesome where males only have sex with the female

Mind orgasms/mindgasms - tuning into the Tantra and the conscious sexuality practices

MMF - male/male/female; a threesome with two men and one woman

Modern (couple) - a code term that refers to a Swinger couple/Lifestyle couple

Newbie - people who are new to the Lifestyle, or to a Lifestyle club or resort

Neo-Tantra - a new Western world style of Tantra

Non-binary - someone who does not identify as solely male or female

Non-monogamy - open relationship

On-premise (SOP)- where sexual activities take place at the event

Open relationship - ethical non-monogamy

Orgasm - coming, cumming, climax

Orgies - a group of people having sex together

Outing - revealing details of one's private life or Lifestyle choices without consent

PDA - public display of affection

PSA - pleasure seeking adult

P-flag parents - supportive parents of a gay child

Pan sexual - attracted to all genders

Plant medicine - traditional medicinal plant that is an important element of indigenous medical systems. Examples include; ayahuasca, magic mushrooms (Psilocybin), cannabis, DMT, kanna, hape

Play - engaging in sexual acts with others

Playroom - an area set up for singles and couples to engage in sexual activities

Playtime - setting up time with others to engage in sexual acts

Pegging - a woman uses a strap-on or dildo to penetrate a male partner in the anus to stimulate the prostate for orgasm

Penis owner - a person who identifies with owning or being born with a penis

Physical orgasms - stimulation of the sexual organs until climax

Poly/Polyamorous - someone who dates others or is in a love bond with more than one person and is honest with all partners

Porcupine back - 2 or 3-day growth of hair on a man's back

Prince Albert - male genital piercing, usually a ring style at the tip of the penis

Psilocybin - a compound found in magic mushrooms; shrooms

Qi - our "life force" energy in traditional Chinese medicine

Queening - when a woman sits on a man's face as he gives her oral pleasure

Queer - a gay, lesbian, bisexual or transgendered person; opposite of a straight person

Role-play - when partners dress up or pretend to be someone else for sexual satisfaction or fun

Rimming - anal licking

Safeword - a prearranged code word to communicate comfort levels in a sexual activity. Common safe words are: green, yellow, and red. Red stops play immediately, yellow pauses play, green is go!

Same room - having sex while in the same room with another couple or person

Service sex - having sex with your spouse out of duty

Sexting - a sexual text, image or video

Shirt cock - men wearing only a t-shirt (and maybe socks)

Sloppy seconds - having sex with a person and then moving on to another person without a cleanup of your intimate parts

S/M - Sadism / Masochism combined; pain for pleasure. Or after a

long day, it could also mean one sleeps, the other masturbates
Soft swing - a couple who never has penetrative sex with others
Somatic therapy - a type of trauma therapy to release emotional and bodily stress trapped in the nervous system
Sport fucking - engaging in sex for casual reasons, sex for fun
Squirting - female ejaculation; gushing a clear and odourless liquid from the pussy
STD - sexually transmitted disease aka old term for STI
STI - sexually transmitted infection aka new term for STD
Straight - heterosexual
Strap-on - a harness worn to hold a dildo
Stunt cock - an extra male who has sex with a female
Swinging/Swinger - a person or couple having sex with others
Sybian - a masturbation device designed that has a saddle-like seat with a vibrating dildo attached. A rider inserts the dildo in a body orifice for internal stimulation
Takeovers - a hotel/cruise/location that is dedicated to having a sexy Adult Only event
Tantra - a slow, meditative form of sex where the end goal may not be physical orgasm
Three-way - a couple plus a single
Threesome - three people having sex together
Tighty whities - snug white underpants for men
Transgender/Trans - someone whose gender identity does not match with the gender assigned at birth
Unicorn - a single woman who plays with couples either together or separately
Vanilla - refers to something that is non-Lifestyle; a monogamous couple/person that has non-kinky sex
Vulva owner - a person who identifies with owning or being born with female genital organs
Voyeur - a single or couple at the back of the room (or off to the side) checking out the action
Water sports - sexual activity in which urine is involved

Sexual Preference Questionnaire

What types of play are you interested in exploring?

Do you and your partner already have a satisfying sex life but you'd both like more novelty and adventure? Or perhaps you want to explore sexual practices and fantasies that can't be done with just the two of you (such as orgies)? Or maybe you are single and you want to express yourself with people who are sex-positive and open-minded?

You've come to the right place. Your fantasy world, however, will continue to be in your mind unless you:
• are honest with yourself about what your fantasies are
• feel safe to share them with your partner
• are open to creating an environment where your fantasies and reality can collide

We've created this extensive quiz to help facilitate the conversation and start the discovery process. When doing the quiz, it's good to check in with your body. Do you get wet, hard or feel energized by some of the questions? Do you get fearful when you think about your partner performing a certain sex act with another? Notice what you are sensing, your body and subconscious mind will guide you to your true desires.

We have compiled the following questions and discussion topics to help you navigate the sometimes difficult task of expressing your true unexplored desires with your partner (or yourself). We encourage you to discuss each one of the ideas as you read through them. There are so many scenarios that we couldn't include every one of them, but we feel it is a good place to start.

Most of the questions only require a yes/no/maybe answer while the discussion topics will require a longer response. Be honest with yourself and your partner. Your understanding of each other is paramount to a successful relationship and lifestyle experience.

You may be surprised to discover that your limits change over time. We suggest revisiting these questions at least 6 months after completing them. It is a great way to see any possible changes in your play style and attitude. Your willingness to accept these limits can smooth your passage through life and give you the means to flourish. If you are not familiar with some of the terms, we suggest that you explore on your favourite search engine together or check out our lexicon or "Alt Dic."

The topics are grouped into three categories:

Play styles

Imagine how you would like to play with others.

Play activities

Consider some of the different types of play (sex acts).

Discussion topics

These are wide and varied and a great time to consider what turns you on (or off). If you are talking about these with your partner make sure you both understand that there will be NO judgment. It is a safe place for you and your partner to share your desires. Some of these topics could be deeply personal. Remember that you will have different responses and that there is no right answer.

PLAY STYLES: What kind of play attracts you?

	YES	NO	MAYBE
Doesn't matter, I'm open to experiment	☐	☐	☐
Couples, soft swing (no swap)	☐	☐	☐
Couples, full swap	☐	☐	☐
Couples, both partners are straight	☐	☐	☐
Couples, female is bi-sexual or curious	☐	☐	☐
Couples, male is bi-sexual or curious	☐	☐	☐
Couples, both are bi-sexual or curious	☐	☐	☐
Single females, straight	☐	☐	☐
Single females, bi-curious	☐	☐	☐
Single females, bi-sexual	☐	☐	☐
Single males, straight	☐	☐	☐
Single males, bi-curious	☐	☐	☐
Single males, bi-sexual	☐	☐	☐
Foursomes	☐	☐	☐
Threesomes	☐	☐	☐
Group sex	☐	☐	☐
Masturbation	☐	☐	☐
Voyeurism	☐	☐	☐

PLAY ACTIVITIES What type of play activities interest you?

	YES	NO	MAYBE
Anal sex	☐	☐	☐
Anal rimming (giving)	☐	☐	☐
Anal rimming (receiving)	☐	☐	☐
Anal toys (giving)	☐	☐	☐
Anal toys (receiving)	☐	☐	☐
Biting	☐	☐	☐
Blindfolds	☐	☐	☐
Bathing together	☐	☐	☐
Bondage (giving)	☐	☐	☐
Bondage (receiving)	☐	☐	☐
Caressing	☐	☐	☐
Chastity device play	☐	☐	☐
Choking (giving)	☐	☐	☐

Questionnaire

	YES	NO	MAYBE
Choking (receiving)	☐	☐	☐
Cuckolding	☐	☐	☐
Cuddling	☐	☐	☐
Climaxing together	☐	☐	☐
Deep throating	☐	☐	☐
Deep breathing together (Breathwork)	☐	☐	☐
Dirty talk	☐	☐	☐
Dressing up	☐	☐	☐
Edging	☐	☐	☐
Electro Stim	☐	☐	☐
Eye contact	☐	☐	☐
Face sitting	☐	☐	☐
Fingering	☐	☐	☐
Fire Play	☐	☐	☐
Fisting	☐	☐	☐
Flirting	☐	☐	☐
Food play	☐	☐	☐
Foot massage	☐	☐	☐
Gags	☐	☐	☐
Genital massage	☐	☐	☐
Golden Shower	☐	☐	☐
Group sex	☐	☐	☐
Hair pulling	☐	☐	☐
Hand jobs	☐	☐	☐
Handcuffs	☐	☐	☐
Homemade porn/Photos	☐	☐	☐
Humiliation	☐	☐	☐
Hot wax massage candle	☐	☐	☐
Internal (G-Spot) stimulation (F)	☐	☐	☐
Internal (Prostate) stimulation (M)	☐	☐	☐
Lap dance	☐	☐	☐
Licking	☐	☐	☐
Making out	☐	☐	☐
Mutual masturbation	☐	☐	☐
Massaging inner thighs	☐	☐	☐

	YES	NO	MAYBE
Neck kissing	☐	☐	☐
Nipple play	☐	☐	☐
Orgasm denial	☐	☐	☐
Phone sex	☐	☐	☐
Period sex	☐	☐	☐
Penis rings	☐	☐	☐
Penis worship	☐	☐	☐
Post-sex shower together	☐	☐	☐
Role playing	☐	☐	☐
Rough Sex - give	☐	☐	☐
Rough Sex - receive	☐	☐	☐
Sexting	☐	☐	☐
Sex games	☐	☐	☐
Sex party	☐	☐	☐
Sex outside	☐	☐	☐
Sex toy play	☐	☐	☐
Sex toy shopping	☐	☐	☐
Slow sex	☐	☐	☐
Spanking	☐	☐	☐
Squirting	☐	☐	☐
Scratching (fingernails or?)	☐	☐	☐
Strap-on play	☐	☐	☐
Tantric sex	☐	☐	☐
Temperature play (cold/hot)	☐	☐	☐
Vulva worship	☐	☐	☐
Watching porn together	☐	☐	☐

DISCUSSION TOPICS

These topics will require more than just a one word answer. They are intended as an invitation for you to have a deeper conversation with your partner.

It is very important to ensure that you create a safe place, and understand that any desires expressed are not used as fodder down the road. You will not receive a true answer if either of you feel any kind of judgment or negative energy.

Questionnaire

- Any major turn-ons/turn-offs?
- Are condoms a must? For which acts?
- Are you into soft swap/full swap play?
- What do you think of "Hot wife" play
- What do you think of "playing alone" with your partner?
- Are you verbal about what you want during play?
- Are you bisexual? Do you have limitations to your play?
- Are you comfortable with couples into cross-dressing?
- Are you into gang bangs. Giver/receiver?
- Are you into BDSM or another form of erotic power exchange?
- Are you into Choking? (breath play)
- Are you into DP? (Double penetration - vagina, anus)
- Are you into DVP? (Double vaginal penetration)
- Are you into fisting?
- Do you like anal play? Do you like to be rimmed? Fingered?
- Do you prefer shaved or natural?
- Do you prefer natural or enhanced breasts?
- As a female, do you enjoy bi males?
- As a female, do you ever fantasized about watching two males play?
- Would you enjoy watching your husband try bi?
- What is your preferred age group? Do you have boundaries? (ie. no younger than my kids, no one my parent's age)
- Do you prefer large or small breasts?
- Complete this statement: "It seems everyone thinks that _____ is great, but I think it is totally overrated."
- Complete this statement: "Nobody seems to like _____, but I love it."
- Complete this statement: "My wildest fantasy is_____"
Do you like photos to be taken during play?
- Do you worry about being "outed"?
- Do you enjoy oral sex? Do you have a preference of giving or receiving?
- Do you enjoy oral sex with the same gender?
- Do you enjoy playing with toys?
- Do you like to use toys when playing with others?
- Do you like "Sexting"?

- Do you like to watch porn? If so, what kind?
- Would you fuck on the first date?
- Do you have any particular fetish?
- Do you have a size preference in your play partner?
- Do you like massages? Giving/receiving?
- Do you like dirty talk?
- Do you like hard pounding sex?
- Do you like hairy men?
- Do you like rough sex?
- Do you like gentle, Tantric sex?
- Lights on or lights off?
- Would you play with anyone who identifies as Trans? Non-binary?
- Do you like to be spanked?
- Do you like to be tied up or bound?
- Do you like to cuddle?
- Do you like to kiss?
- Do you like to role play with your partner?
- Do you like orgies?
- Do you play during a menstrual cycle?
- Do you prefer slow and sensual or fast and furious?
- Do you prefer to stay within your own ethnicity?
- During play, is kissing allowed?
- Have you ever been to an adult theater, glory hole or tried "Dogging"?
- Do you like to masturbate for, or with, a member of the same sex?
- Have you ever wanted to or would you ever be in a meaningful relationship with more than one person? (Polyamory)
- How do you feel about "pegging"? Would you receive (male) / give (female)?
- How do you feel about hook ups (aka one night stands)?
- How do you feel about playing somewhere public?
- How do you feel about "water sports"? (Body fluid play)
- Is bigger better?
- What do you think of "Hall passes"?
- Is there anything sexual you want reserved for just your partner?
- Which activities aren't allowed with you?
- Do you have a preferred body type?

- Do you have a favorite toy?
- What do you find sexy in a partner?
- What do you like most about men?
- What do you like most about women?
- What intrigues you right now sexually?
- What is a mood killer during play?
- Do you have a sexual fantasy you haven't fulfilled? Will you share?
- What is too "kinky" for you?
- What is your guilty pleasure?
- Do you have a favorite sexual position?
- When you are at a party, do you enjoy the act of voyeurism? How do you feel about being watched?
- When is your favourite time of day for sex?
- When playing with another female (solo or with your partner) do you like them to be dominant or submissive?
- Do you enjoy a man cumming on your body? If so, where?
- Would you enjoy being a unicorn for a couple?
- Would you ever consider switching out your partner for a night?
- Would you describe yourself as dominant or submissive?
- Would you prefer new and casual partners or having regular play partners?

NOTES / THOUGHTS / WISH LIST

Reading

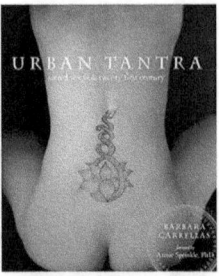

URBAN TANTRA - Barbara Carrellas
With a juicy mix of erotic how-to and plea-sure-centered spiritual wisdom, acclaimed sex educator Barbara Carrellas radically updates the ancient practice of Tantra for modern sexual ex-plorers desiring to push past their edge in search of the great cosmic orgasm. ISBN-10: 1587612909

The Enlightened Sex Manual - David Deida
For men and women, singles and couples of every sexual orientation, The Enlightened Sex Manual provides a complete program for sustaining "whole-body recognition of love's light" in the wild play of sexuality. **Finding God Through Sex** is another great one in his series
ASIN: B001HBI792

The Master Key: Qigong Secrets for Vitality, Love, and Wisdom - Robert Peng
Eastern energy systems like Qigong can be dif-ficult for Westerners to grasp because of the unique vocabulary and unfamiliar metaphors employed. Peng has organized this ancient Chi-nese teaching in a way that puts it squarely with-in Western comfort zones.
ISBN-10: 1622031393

Stepping Off the Relationship Escalator: Uncom-mon Love and Life - Amy Gahran
Most people assume that healthy or serious rela-tionships which involve romance and sex are sup-posed to follow these steps: from attraction and dating, through exclusivity and living together, to marriage that ideally lasts a lifetime. That's what's called the traditional "Relationship Escalator."

Consulting • Mentorship • Other Resources

Kandace and Gregory aka Maggie and Josh

We offer personal counselling and mentorship for singles, couples and other relationship configurations. Are you ready for something more in your sexual relationship? Give yourself permission to expand your sexuality in the world around you.

Find us at: **www.evolutionarysex.org**
For more information: **info@evolutionarysex.org**

Luna Ceovelli

Luna is a certified systemic and family constellations facilitator and a holistic coach whose mission is to create safe transformational spaces for people to experience the magnificent truth of who they really are. To book a discovery call or learn more send a message to 1 (604) 727-4329,
or email me at **lunaceovelli@gmail.com**

Raynefyre authentic intimacy facilitator.

Raynefyre travels internationally to playfully offer trauma informed, erotic experiences with a focus on curious, whole body exploration and expanding sexual pleasure. In service to queer-hearted women, trans and gender nonconforming folks, they support embodiment through breath, movement, touch and play.

For more info or to book: **love@raynefyre.ca**

N.A.P.S./ Todd Ritchey
Finally Neuroscience and plant medicine unite. Our model is based on cutting edge brain science, and offers the tools and a method for understanding the psychedelic experience within the context of healing the debilitating patterns that hold us back from living fully. - **napsmycology.com**

EVOLUTIONARYSEX'g

Lifestyle Websites and Apps

www.lifestylelounge.com

www.kasidie.com

www.clubeden.ca

We have been members of these sites since they began.

www.feeld.com

Feeld is a dating app for exploration, curiosity and pleasure. Join solo or with a partner to find lovers and friends.

Available on the Apple store or Google Play

www.itlenm.com - The Ethical Non Monogamy Dating App you have been searching for. ITL ENM is purposefully built for all relationship types and dynamics. Free to Join & Use!

Available on the Apple store or Google Play

Travel

www.LLVClub.com

At Luxury Lifestyle Vacations you'll become part of a worldwide family of travelers, risk takers and lovers of life. Our exclusive take-overs of adults only all inclusive resorts bring dreams into reality for open-minded couples and adventurous singles.

Desire Resorts - www.desire-resort.com

A couples only oasis located just South of Cancun.

Hedonism Resort - www.hedonism.com

Hedonism II is one of the most famous clothing optional resorts in the world. Located in Negril, Jamaica, Hedo is a lifestyle-friendly, clothing-optional beach resort where you can do pretty much what you want when you want.

Temptations Resorts - www.temptation-experience.com

Temptation Adults Only Resorts and Cruises offer one-of-a-kind "Playgrounds for Grown-Ups", both on land and at sea. For the sexy and adventurous!

Spiritual retreats

Rythmia Life Advancement Center | Ayahuasca Retreat Center

Rythmia is an all-inclusive, luxury medically-licensed plant medicine center located in beautiful Guanacaste, Costa Rica. **www.rythmia.com**

Music

Our current favorite Spotify playlists include:
G's spiritual Trance / Peaceful Growth / Shamanic Journey / Ananda

Podcasts

Sex with Dr. Jess

Dr. Jess is a Toronto-based sexologist (PhD), author and television personality. An award-winning speaker, Jess has worked with thousands of couples from all corners of the globe **www.sexwithdrjess.com**

Sex w/ Emily

Doctor of Human Sexuality, Emily Morse, is on a mission to liberate the conversation about sex and pleasure. **www.sexwithemily.com**

Shameless Sex

Together, Amy and April combined forces to create the Shameless Sex Podcast, inspiring radical self-love, sexual empowerment, and shame-free intimacy. **www.shamelesssex.com**

Favorite Toys

Feeldoe® Original Strapless Dildos

The world's first and original strapless strap-on double dildos.
www.feeldoe.com

Erossica

Erosscia turns your electric electric toothbrush into a luxury & discreet vibrator. Body safe, Erosscia has been elected the most innovative massager.
www.erosscia.com

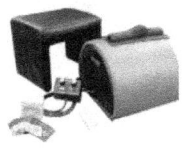

Sybian

Sybian is the most sophisticated sexual aid available. Its unparalleled simplistic design provides varied stimulation and maximum pleasure; with easy to use controls. **www.sybian.com**